THE STORY OF
KENT

THE STORY OF
KENT
ANNE PETRIE

For all my wonderful children and grandchildren

First published 2017

The History Press
The Mill, Brimscombe Port
Stroud, Gloucestershire, GL5 2QG
www.thehistorypress.co.uk

British Library Cataloguing in Publication Data.
A catalogue record for this book is available from the British Library.

ISBN 978 0 7509 6747 1

Typesetting and origination by The History Press
Printed and bound in Great Britain by TJ International Ltd

CONTENTS

ACKNOWLEDGEMENTS

This book could not have been written without the generously given help and time of many people.

Roger Parker and Jon Spence corrected my mistakes, improved my grammar, suggested sources and made helpful criticisms about the way the story is put together. Any remaining errors are mine alone.

Anne Thompson, supported and chauffeured by husband Alan, took most of the photographs, risking sunstroke, braving gale-force winds on the Kent coast and finding her way to impossibly remote sites. She was assisted in editing the pictures by Matt Gore. Thanks are also due to Bill Ridley for finding the elusive oast house, to Andrew Sweeney for permission to use photos from St Leonard's church and to Elizabeth Pearson and Alison Noyes for information about Dungeness.

The staff at Hythe library dealt uncomplainingly with the huge quantity of books I ordered over the course of a year, and were always ready to help with any queries. Finally, I am hugely indebted to the authors of all those books, whose research forms the basis of this story.

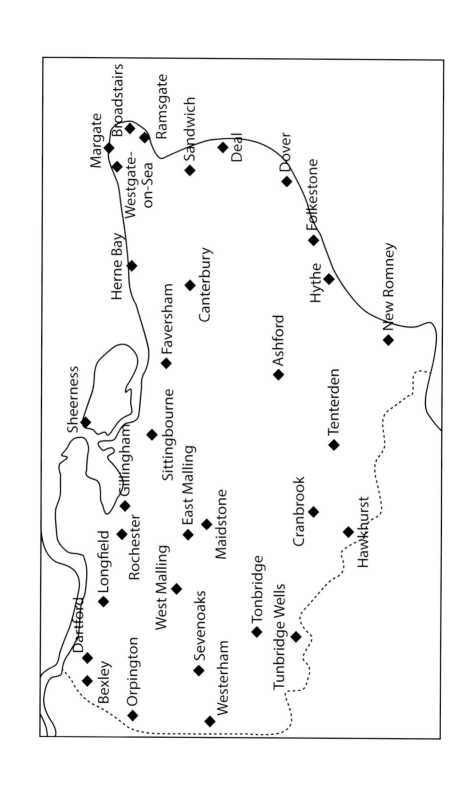

One

THE FIRST MILLENNIUM

Dawn, on an early autumn day on the south coast of Kent, high up on the White Cliffs above Dover: a man on horseback shades his eyes as he scans the horizon. He strains forward as the first rays of the rising sun strike the grey sea. He thinks he spots movement. A few minutes later he is sure. He turns and gives the signal to his comrades. They mount their horses, javelins at the ready and wait.

But the ships stop short, out of range of their weapons. They drop anchor and ride the waves for hours, also waiting. Men come and go from the ships and can clearly be seen conferring with their leader. They wave their arms and point and nod, but not a word can be heard. It would make no difference if they spoke as clearly as bells, for they talk in a tongue which is strange to the men on the cliffs.

When the sun is well up, other ships appear, manned with soldiers in heavy leather and metal armour and helmets. But still the ships do not land. They weigh anchor and sail east along the coast.

The man on horseback gives the order and his army moves off in the same direction, mounted chieftains followed by their cavalry, men in chariots, foot soldiers bringing up the rear. They march along the high undulating ground which drops eventually to the flat stretches of beach that lie to the east. Here the ships drop anchor again and the armoured men start to disembark.

At first it is laughably easy to pick them off. The sea is breathtakingly cold, the foreign men cannot stand on the slippery shingle of the sea bed, and waist-deep in water their heavy armour weighs them down. They slide, stumble and fall, losing their weapons and cursing. The waves break red on the shore. Then some of the smaller, strange-looking ships of the alien fleet break away. The crew start to use oars to bring them close inshore and a hail of arrows is directed at the beach. Great machines on the decks hurl rocks with deadly accuracy at the defenders. The foreign soldiers, in shallower water, flounder less, start to reach the beach and to cut down their enemies. The islanders are outnumbered and out-armed and they do the only sensible thing – retreat.

Such was the first day of the first known attempted invasion of Britain, the first of many which, for the next two millennia, put Kent on the front line of the defence of the nation.

In 55 BC, Julius Caesar, fresh from subduing the Gauls, had turned his eyes towards Britain. He wrote later that he thought the Britons were helping the Gauls, and that although it was the wrong time of year for a full-scale invasion, he would like to get a feel for the place and its people. Others have

A plaque on the shingle beach at Walmer commemorates Caesar's first landing in 55 BC. (Anne Thompson)

attributed his mission to a desire to see whether Britain was rich enough to be worth invading (he was heavily in debt) or to a need to bolster his reputation as a soldier at home. The Britons knew none of this: they just got wind that he was gathering troops on the other side of the Channel.

Caesar had sent a spy ahead of him, who sailed the Kent coast but did not land. The Roman fleet of about a hundred ships set sail for Dover, which must have been identified as a good natural harbour, but sensibly Caesar did not disembark as he could see the native tribes gathered on the cliffs above, poised to shower javelins down on his army. He waited a while, anchored in deep water, for more of his fleet to catch up, and sailed along the coast to an open beach, probably at Walmer. The Kentish tribes followed him along the cliffs and put up fierce resistance on the shore. It was not they, however, but the British weather which finally persuaded Caesar to retreat. An autumn storm seriously damaged the Roman fleet. With winter approaching, Caesar exercised his discretion and sailed back to Gaul. He would be back.

The operation was a propaganda success for Caesar and the next year, better armed and better prepared, he tried again with, according to him, no fewer than 800 vessels. He landed again at Walmer, and this time was unopposed. Caesar, never afraid to blow his own trumpet, wrote that the tribes were 'terrified by the vast number of ships', but it may be that they were just mustering their forces.

He took some of his crack troops and marched inland, meeting and rebuffing Kentish warriors on the way. After a brief hiatus to repair some storm-damaged ships, he continued his march about ten days later. Now he met the massed forces of the Britons, from north of the Thames as well as from Kent. The Britons risked a few skirmishes, but soon realised that they could not win in a pitched battle and tried guerrilla tactics instead. Undeterred, Caesar forged ahead until he reached the Thames, where he is said to have used an elephant to help his troops cross the heavily defended river.

At this point, some of the British tribes started to make their peace with Caesar, but the four leaders of the Kentish tribes staged a diversionary attack on the Walmer beachhead to try to draw Caesar off. It failed, and they reluctantly agreed to surrender. They gave hostages, and agreed to pay tribute money to Rome.

On a lonely stretch of the Medway, a simple stone near the hamlet of Burham marks the place where the Roman army defeated the British tribes in 54 BC. It is regarded by some as second only to the Battle of Hastings in importance for England. (Anne Thompson)

Caesar then sailed back to Gaul, and left not a single soldier to enforce the agreement, which was almost certainly ignored once the Romans had put the English Channel between the two armies.

The status quo remained largely intact for the next ninety years. True, the Emperor Augustus did plan to re-invade on several occasions but he either changed his mind or was distracted by other matters. Later Caligula, an idiosyncratic emperor to say the least, also tried. He drew up his troops in battle formation facing the Channel and ordered them to attack the sea. This unique approach did not work. It fell to his successor, Claudius, to make the definitive invasion.

By the AD 40s, a fierce dynastic power struggle had developed in Britain. Verica, one of the kings deposed in the tussle, appealed for help to Claudius, who coincidentally needed a decent military victory to boost his rather lacklustre image. Not a soldier himself, he put Aulus Plautius, a distinguished senator, in charge of four legions, and despatched them to the shores of Gaul. Sailing from Boulogne, the troops landed at Richborough in East Kent: no sailing up and down the Channel this time, but a direct approach to a known safe harbour. This was an immaculately planned operation.

The Romans' progress inland was unstoppable. On the Medway, near Rochester, a substantial British force led by the chieftain Caractacus met them, but after two days was defeated and the Romans pushed on to the Thames. The army left behind in Kent quickly established peaceable terms with the tribes. In the rest of the country, the Romans consolidated their takeover, which was to endure for nearly 400 years.

Occupation by a foreign power had its compensations. Caesar had reported that Kent, or *Cantium,* was thickly studded with farmsteads and that its people were the 'most civilised' of the whole island. They proved themselves eager to become even more 'civilised'. Although subsistence farmers carried on living in their round thatched huts, the slightly better-off started building themselves the new Roman-style rectangular cottages on stone foundations. These homes of three to five rooms have been excavated at Burham, Sandwich, Cobham Park and Charing. Country villas were also built, ranging from small farmhouses to huge luxury residences, often the homes not of Romans, but of the British elite, who enthusiastically adopted the Roman lifestyle. One of the first to be built was at Lullingstone, near Eynsford. Conveniently situated near Watling Street, the main Roman road to London, Canterbury and Rochester, the building was started in around AD 80. Seventy years later it was extended and a centrally heated bath block was added. Central heating was later installed throughout the villa, and the dining room was remodelled and given a fine mosaic floor with depictions of the gods. One room was used as both a pagan shrine, and, later, as a Christian chapel, one of the earliest in Britain.

Another, slightly later villa, at Orpington, has been partly conserved, although most of the surrounding estate buildings are now under Orpington railway station. It was built with flint walls and a tiled roof. Off the single corridor, five rooms faced south-east, overlooking the scenic valley of the River Cray. This relatively humble building was also later enlarged and improved by adding extensions and installing central heating. Home improvements were *de rigueur* for the Romano-Briton on the make.

Apart from its agriculture, *Cantium* was also an important industrial area in early Roman times. The vast machinery of the Roman military needed iron and the raw materials of ore and hardwood timber to make charcoal were easily available in the Weald of Kent. The iron-working sites here were hugely productive. It has been estimated that one, at Bardown, had an annual output of 100 to 200 tonnes.

Pottery manufacture in the county was also on an industrial scale, and much of it must have been intended for outside Kent. Again, the industry was probably meeting military needs. Production was centred in Eccles, the Medway marshes and in Canterbury. These sites also made tiles for use in the new residences which were springing up in towns as well as rural areas.

One of these towns was Canterbury, which developed from an Iron Age settlement into a major urban centre. Early in their occupation there, the Romans started introducing their own culture. Tribal huts were removed and replaced and by AD 90 there was a timber theatre in the settlement. A little later, a full-scale expansion programme imposed a planned street system and the typical Roman public buildings – forum, basilica, baths and temples. Later still, in about AD 210, the theatre was rebuilt in stone and seems to have seated an audience of up to 7,000, one of the largest in all Roman Britain. Canterbury, *Durovernum* to the Romans, was an important trade, social and religious centre.

The other Iron Age site which attracted the Romans was at Rochester, but apart from its defences, little excavation has been done and not much is known about the city in Roman times.

Major excavations have, however, been carried out at Dover, which developed from a tiny settlement into a major naval base under Roman rule. Then, the estuary of the now peaceful little River Dour covered most of what is now Dover's town centre. It provided the only break in 20km of steep cliffs, and it was on the banks of this tidal delta that the Romans built the base for the *Classis Britannica* fleet. This supported the army, policed the Channel and seems also to have been involved in the transportation of iron. Its base at Dover, known to the Romans as *Dubris*, comprised an HQ building, barrack blocks and granaries, accessed through four gates in the massive walls. Nearby were quays, a harbour wall, and on the White Cliffs above, a lighthouse, or *pharos*.

A little later, a smart new hotel for cross-Channel visitors was built, with a state-of-the-art central heating system and elegantly decorated rooms. It is still open to visitors, although not to overnight guests, as the Roman Painted House in Dover town centre.

Dover had succeeded Richborough (*Rutupiae*) as the home port of the *Classis Britannica*. The beachhead there was developed into a large supply depot, with a typical Roman grid street pattern dividing the area up into blocks containing stores, granaries, administrative buildings and sleeping quarters. The depot lasted for about fifty years, but before it was abandoned, a huge monument to the invasion was erected, over 26m tall, encased in Carrara marble and decorated with bronze statues. In the flat, featureless landscape, it must have been visible for miles around.

Richborough became a backwater for a couple of hundred years, but was heavily fortified in the third century, using the stone from the demolished monument as building material. It was one of a string of forts stretching

The remains of the Roman *pharos* or lighthouse at Dover. Its stones were used in about AD 1000 to build the church of St Mary in Castro, which can be seen behind it. (Anne Thompson)

The massive remains of Richborough Roman fort. Perhaps the most symbolically important of all Roman sites in Britain, it witnessed both the beginning and the end of Roman rule. (Anne Thompson)

along the coast. During the second half of the third century the whole Roman Empire was under threat, weakened by civil war and facing attacks by barbarian tribes. England was protected from raids in the north by Hadrian's Wall, but lacked similar defences in the south.

To remedy the problem, huge square forts were built at Richborough, Dover, Reculver and Lympne, and other coastal sites outside Kent, garrisoned and prepared to withstand long sieges. On a modern map, only Reculver and Dover are still on the coast. Lympne and Richborough have long since been separated from the sea, cut off by the silt and shingle relentlessly swept along the English Channel. Reculver was once at the end of the Wantsum Channel, nearly 5km wide in places, which separated the Isle of Thanet from the mainland, and which provided a convenient short cut for shipping travelling from London to the continent. It, too, silted up in the Middle Ages, and Thanet is now an isle in name only.

The Roman fort at Lympne, now known as Stutfall Castle. Once on the coast, the remains are now several kilometres inland and are slipping inexorably downhill. (Anne Thompson)

The towns, settlements, forts and depots were all linked by that supreme achievement of Roman civilisation, the paved road. Their development started almost immediately after the invasion, to meet military needs, with the road through Canterbury to London, later known as Watling Street. It originally began at Richborough, though this was later changed to Dover, and after passing through Canterbury proceeded to Rochester, then by bridge over the Medway to Strood. Then it crossed the rivers Darent and Cray before reaching London via Greenwich.

A network of roads supported this artery. There was a road from Lympne to Canterbury, from Dover to Richborough, one from Reculver to Canterbury, and a main road from Rochester to the Weald and Hastings. An offshoot of this formed the road which led to Lympne, and thence to Dover. Transport and communications during the Roman occupation were faster and easier than they would be again until Victorian times.

The roads and much else of Roman civilisation fell into disrepair and eventual ruin when the Romans left in AD 410. The threat to the empire from the north European tribes did not go away, and successive emperors had been withdrawing troops to redeploy them in Gaul and elsewhere for over twenty years. Eventually the Emperor Honorius told Britain that it was now responsible for its own defence. The last troops left, as they had arrived, through Richborough, and it is likely that the richest civilians went with them. They had long since abandoned their great country villas for the security of the towns.

The era that followed is generally referred to as the Dark Ages, not just because it was nasty, brutish and pagan, although it was undoubtedly all those things, but because what happened then is now dim and indistinct. Sources are unclear, contradictory and full of unexplained allusions which defy a single interpretation, and some accounts were written many, many years after the events they purport to describe. The various tribes that invaded and settled in England are usually referred to under the umbrella description 'Anglo-Saxon', but there were, as well as Angles and Saxons, also many Jutes, who particularly favoured Kent. Whatever their origins, they did not bring with them the civilising influences that had characterised the Roman occupation.

In about AD 425, a strong English king, Vortigern, emerged from the chaotic vacuum left by Rome. He may, or may not, have invited the Jutish (or maybe Saxon) brothers Hengist and Horsa, mercenary soldiers, to help him fight the Picts. They probably arrived in AD 446. The brothers' story rests primarily on an account by the Venerable Bede written 300 years later, but if we accept the myth, then Hengist, having traitorously despatched Vortigern and his son, went on to become the first ruler of the kingdom of Kent.

He was succeeded by his son (or possibly his grandson) Aesc, and after a few rather shadowy figures, eventually, in about AD 589, by Aethelbert. Here at last is a man who is fully described in the historical records. Under his leadership, Kent emerged as a fully fledged kingdom, with a royal house, written laws, and the full machinery of government. He was also the first English king to be baptised, making Kent the first Christian kingdom in Britain.

Christianity had been legalised in the Roman Empire in AD 313 and some Romano-Britons had converted. The Anglo-Saxon invaders were pagans, and by the time of Aethelbert, Christian believers only existed in the west of Britain, where their Church had developed separately from the Church of Rome.

Aethelbert had married a Christian princess, Bertha, who arrived from Paris with her chaplain, the Frankish bishop Liudhard. Aethelbert allowed them to use the old Romano-British church of St Martin's in Canterbury for their devotions. He then either invited Christian missionaries to Kent, or they were sent uninvited by Pope Gregory I. In any event, a Benedictine monk called Augustine and about forty followers landed in Thanet in AD 597. Aethelbert allowed them to preach in Canterbury, his capital, and Christianity became the fashionable club to join after the conversion of the king. The fact that the Church supported his kingship may have been a factor in Aethebert's decision. Augustine established bishoprics at

St Martin's church, Canterbury, is England's oldest parish church still regularly used for Christian worship. (Anne Thompson)

Canterbury and Rochester and became Archbishop of Canterbury himself, dying in AD 604. Both he and Queen Bertha were later venerated as saints.

Aristocratic women, particularly, took an interest in and sometimes founded religious houses. They were a safe haven for widowed queens, chaste princesses and other noble ladies. They followed the example of Aethelburga, the daughter of Aethelbert and Bertha. She had made the obligatory dynastic marriage to King Edwin of Northumbria, converted him to Christianity and borne him several children. On his death in battle, pausing only to collect most of his treasure, she fled back to Kent. There she founded the religious house at Lyminge where she was abbess until her death in 647.

This was a convenient arrangement for her family. Aethelburga was in a position of dignity befitting her status, comfortable, and seen to be a devoted Christian. Just as it was the function of royal men to acquire land and power, it was the function of royal women to serve: by marrying

A plaque on the wall of Lyminge church marks the burial place of St Aethelburga (now the accepted spelling of her name). It is near the recently excavated double monastery which she founded. (Anne Thompson)

advantageously, by producing heirs and by supporting the Church which propped up the notion of kingship.

Another queen, Sexburgha, was married to a grandson of Aethelbert. During her husband's lifetime she had founded the convent of Minster-in-Sheppey. This was a family tradition: her sister Aethelreda had also founded a nunnery at Ely. Sexburgha retired to her convent when she was widowed, but despite its isolated location, it was not secluded enough for her and she moved to her sister's establishment instead. Aethelreda died, and although she desired only a quiet life, Sexburgha was obliged to become abbess in her place. Meanwhile, her widowed daughter Ermenilda took over as abbess at Minster-in-Sheppey. All these women were subsequently venerated as saints.

It is, in fact, nigh on impossible to find an Anglo-Saxon woman saint from Kent who was not of royal descent. Similarly, it was almost impossible to become Archbishop of Canterbury without becoming a saint as well. The first twelve to hold the post were all later venerated, all except Wighard who died of the plague before he could be consecrated.

The process of canonisation by the Pope was not introduced until AD 993, and the only criterion for sainthood, apart from a reputedly holy life or martyrdom, was that a miracle should have been attributed to the deceased. It must also be said that the presence of saintly relics in a minster church or cathedral did nothing to harm its revenues from pilgrims.

The Christian Aethelbert was succeeded by a series of kings whose most notable characteristic was their unchristian behaviour. His son Eadbald celebrated his succession to the throne of Kent by rejecting Christianity and marrying his own stepmother. Eadbald's son, Eorcenbert, illegally excluded his own nephews from the succession in order to gain power. His heir Egbert had his nephews murdered to secure the kingship. The next king, Lothar, took the throne by force, but was driven into exile by his even more violent and hot-headed nephew Eadric. He in turn was dethroned by an outsider from Wessex, Mul, who was so disliked by his people that they set fire to the building in Canterbury in which he was hiding and burnt him to death.

The next two kings of Kent only lasted a few months each, but some stability was restored by Wihtred, who ruled Kent from AD 691 to AD 725.

He updated the law code introduced by Aethelbert and, as a devout Christian, exempted the Church from taxation. On his death, he nominated three co-kings to rule in his place and avoid a repetition of the internecine fighting which had so marred the previous hundred years.

The successors to the co-kings were outsiders, chosen by the nobles of England. The choice of Eanmund in AD 762 annoyed Offa, the King of Mercia, so much that he invaded Kent and installed his own man. The people of Kent fought back, but the kingdom was effectively ruled by puppet kings under the thumb of Mercia for the next eighty years. The last of these, Baldred, was deposed by the King of Wessex in AD 825 and the autonomous kingdom of Kent effectively ceased to exist. It was now a sub-kingdom of Wessex. In AD 860 even that small consolation vanished and Kent became a full province of Wessex. However, it was during this time that the attention of the English kings began to be diverted away from fighting each other and towards fighting a common enemy – the Vikings.

Kent was an attractive target for these Norwegian and Danish raiders as its wealthy monasteries with their minster churches were often located conveniently near to the coast. In AD 804, the nuns of Lyminge sought refuge in Canterbury to escape the attackers, and in AD 811 Kentish forces repelled a Viking onslaught on the convent church of the Isle of Sheppey. In AD 841, the *Anglo-Saxon Chronicle* tells us that 'Ealdorman Herebryht was killed by heathen men and many of the people of Romney Marsh with him'.

The Vikings were not there to civilise, like the Romans, or settle like the Anglo-Saxons. They were there to take what they could, as quickly as they could and to move on to the next target. They mounted hit-and-run raids: a landing made, the locals taken on and defeated, the place ransacked and the raiders went off with their plunder. They rarely stayed for more than a few weeks and seldom went more than 25km inland. This was just a foretaste of what was to come.

By AD 850 the raiders had grown more confident and, to avoid the rigours of the Scandinavian winter, spent the cold season in Kent, on the Isle of Thanet. Fifteen years later, the small groups of longboats and their crews had swelled to become what the *Anglo-Saxon Chronicle* called 'The Great Heathen Army'. For the next thirty years, 3,000 armed men roamed the country, killing, pillaging and burning at will.

At this desperate time, salvation arrived in the form of King Alfred of Wessex (he wasn't 'the Great' until later). Crowned in AD 871, he at first appeased the invaders by buying them off, but when this approach failed, he went on the offensive and in AD 885 drove off a Viking army which had been besieging Rochester. Seven years later he dispersed enemy encampments at Appledore on the Romney Marsh and at Milton Regis, near Sittingbourne. The Vikings, although claiming the land north of the Thames as the Danelaw, never conquered Wessex and its province of Kent.

Alfred's victories brought freedom from Viking attack in the south, giving time and leisure for his successors to revive the ancient custom of fighting each other. Occupied in this way, and sometimes in fighting the Welsh and Scots too, they largely left Kent alone. Ignored by the ruling elite, by the tenth century, it was in a state of economic stagnation, but the end of the century saw a revival of its fortunes. Dover, particularly, flourished, and, since it had a mint, probably also had a royal patron. In the early eleventh century the defences on its eastern cliffs were refurbished, including the building of a church with walls suspiciously massive for a place of worship, St Mary in Castro.

The figurehead of the replica Viking ship *Hugin* on display at Pegwell Bay, near Ramsgate. The ship was sailed from Denmark in 1949. Behind it is the 'Armada beacon', one of a string erected in 1988 to mark the quarter centenary of the event. (Anne Thompson)

Defences were necessary, because the Vikings were back and were now attacking Kent from the sea. Sandwich was hit many times, its large haven being a favoured anchorage for the Anglo-Saxon fleet, and Canterbury was sacked in 1011. This time the raids ended with victory for the Danes and the coronation of Cnut as King of all England in AD 1017. Cnut consolidated his victory by marrying Emma, the widow of Aethelred the Unready (it meant 'ill-advised' then), who had died of wounds while resisting the Vikings. Their son Harthacnut succeeded, but his rule was cut short after two years when he dropped dead at a wedding in Lambeth after a heavy drinking session. His half-brother, Edward, the son of Aethelred and Emma, took over. He is known to history as Edward the Confessor.

The reaction of the ordinary people of Kent to these invasions, battles, upheavals and religious conversions is not recorded, but we know a little of how they lived away from the hurly-burly of the power struggles.

When the Romans left Kent, society collapsed. People stopped using coinage and returned to a barter economy. Without the buying power of the Roman military, the great pottery industries ceased trading and the Wealden iron works fell into decay. Urban life seems to have come to an end. Rochester and Dover were abandoned and Canterbury was returned to agriculture. Elsewhere there is evidence of comprehensive depopulation.

What happened to the Romano-British was, according to the *Anglo-Saxon Chronicle*, either wholesale butchery or lifelong slavery at the hands of the invaders. The lack of archaeological evidence for their survival bears this out. The incomers settled on the prime farmland that had been cultivated under the Romans, and carried on with the practices of their predecessors – mixed farming together with fishing and trading in coastal settlements. They had close trading links with both their nearest continental neighbour, Francia, and with southern Scandinavia. Trade at this time was mostly imports of pottery in exchange for slaves, these probably being the remnants of the Romano-British people.

The arrival of Aethelbert with his law codes and of the Christian Church with its own rules set in place a hierarchical society with the king at the very top. Under the king were *eorls* (well-born freemen), *coerls* (ordinary freemen), and *laets* (labourers). At the very bottom of the pile were the slaves. Even the king, Aethelbert, had his place in a hierarchy of his own, his largely imaginary family tree, which proved his descent from the Germanic war god, Woden.

The kingdom of Kent was divided into administrative areas called lathes, and sometime in the ninth or tenth century the lathes were subdivided into hundreds, although the boundaries were not fixed until much later. Each hundred had its own court or meeting place to discuss administrative matters and to deal with tenancy and land dispute cases.

Land ownership became increasingly important, and the major landowner, apart from the king, was the Church. Monastic houses assembled around them buildings and industries, creating major sites – minsters – which were the size of, and functioned as, small towns. The double monastery (for both men and women) at Lyminge had, as well as domestic areas and a church, sites for agricultural processing, metalworking, smelting, smithing, textile manufacture, leatherworking and grain processing. The houses were rich. The Lyminge house obtained a regular supply of oysters and fish from its Romney Marsh estates and the convent of Minster-in-Sheppey, much favoured by aristocratic ladies, owned at least three ships trading out of Fordwich, London and Sarre.

Each minster had a least one church within its precincts and St Augustine's Monastery at Canterbury had three by the mid-seventh century. Built at first of wood, the seventh century saw a return to the use of stone as a building material, and Roman brick and tiles were often recycled and incorporated in the construction.

Canterbury had been used by Aethelbert as his capital, and during his reign it slowly emerged as the centre of economic and political affairs. With the building of the cathedral it became the head of ecclesiastical government as well. It also had its own mint, as did Rochester and Dover, the revival of the use of coinage being sure evidence of economic recovery.

The Viking raids of the ninth and tenth centuries put a temporary halt to this revival, but by the time of Cnut, growth was underway again. New streets sprang up in Canterbury, lined with commercial premises, and its population was estimated to be about 8,000 at the beginning of the eleventh century. Some of these people were employed in a new ceramics industry, producing pots and tiles. More churches were built and major construction work was done at the cathedral, making it one of the largest churches in northern Europe.

As well as the established urban sites of Canterbury, Dover and Rochester, coastal settlements such as Sandwich, Hythe and Romney began to mature into towns, and to profit from more settled times by developing havens and fishing industries. Hythe was even minting its own coins by AD 1048. These towns were to develop into the politically and economically powerful Confederation of the Cinque Ports.

Kent had emerged as a thriving community from over 1,000 years of invasion and conquest, by the Romans, the Angles, the Saxons, the Jutes and by the Vikings. It had been pagan, Christian, then pagan again and finally settled for Christianity. It had known subjugation, slavery, autonomy and neglect. Now its strong economic, religious and geographical position made it of particular interest to the next invasion that its people would face, from just across the Channel in Normandy.

Two

WHAT THE NORMANS DID FOR KENT

The saintly Edward the Confessor died without sons and was succeeded to the throne of England by Harold Godwinson, elected in January 1066 by an assembly of the great and the good of England. His reign would not last the year. Another man believed, or said he did, that the Confessor had promised him the throne. He was the bastard descendant of Viking pirates, William, Duke of Normandy. Furious that Harold had appropriated his inheritance, William spent the summer of 1066 gathering his forces and in early autumn was ready to take what he claimed was rightfully his. Delayed initially by poor weather, he finally set sail across the Channel on 27 September. The story and outcome of the bloody and hard-fought battle near Hastings needs no retelling.

The victor, but not yet king, William needed to consolidate his position and to get to London, the seat of power. He also needed to feed and shelter his army, numbering about 5,000 men. More than anything else, he needed to assert his supremacy and crush the English people.

He had time on his side, as there was no organised opposition. He decided not to march directly to London, but to travel through Kent, where some strategic towns and ports could be picked off en route. He took the old Roman road east from Hastings towards Tenterden and Ashford. At Tenterden he sent a detachment of men south to the port of Romney. On 29 September some of his men had been blown ashore there and had been slaughtered by the townsfolk. William wanted this first example of his justice to make an impact, and although exactly what happened at Romney is not recorded, it was brutal enough to strike terror into the rest of the county.

NEAR THIS SPOT IN THE YEAR 1067. BY ANCIENT TRADITION THE MEN of KENT AND KENTISH MEN. CARRYING BOUGHS ON THEIR SHOULDERS AND SWORDS IN THEIR HANDS. MET THE INVADER. WILLIAM. DUKE of NORMANDY. THEY OFFERED PEACE IF HE WOULD GRANT THEIR ANCIENT RIGHTS AND LIBERTIES OTHERWISE WAR AND THAT MOST DEADLY. THEIR REQUEST WAS GRANTED AND FROM THAT DAY THE MOTTO OF KENT HAS BEEN 'INVICTA'. MEANING UNCONQUERED.

This monument to the legendary meeting between William the Conqueror and the branch-bearing inhabitants of Kent originally stood near the old A2 road – the Roman Watling Street. When the road was widened it was moved to the church of St Peter and St Paul in Swanscombe. (Anne Thompson)

From Tenterden William marched eastward to Dover. News of his actions at Romney had preceded him, and Dover surrendered immediately, but the town was burned to the ground anyway. William spent some time there fortifying it to his own specifications. It must have seemed like divine retribution to the people of Dover when the Norman army was visited with an outbreak of dysentery.

Undeterred, William pressed on to Canterbury, which also sensibly surrendered immediately, and then, after recovering from dysentery himself, proceeded to London. Legend has it that, en route, while marching along Watling Street, he encountered a host of locals armed only with tree branches and swords. They offered peace if William would protect their ancient rights and liberties. William agreed and from that day the county adopted the motto *Invicta*, undefeated. It makes a pretty, if far-fetched, story.

On Christmas Day, 1066, in Westminster Abbey, William was crowned by the Archbishop of York. The Archbishop of Canterbury, Stigand, who would have been expected to perform the deed, was disqualified as he had been excommunicated by five successive popes for illegally holding both the see of Canterbury and that of Winchester at the same time. He was infamous for being both very lazy and very rich at the cost of the Church; most of his own bishops avoided him if they could.

Within three months of his coronation, William felt secure enough to return to Normandy, leaving Kent under the control of his half-brother, Odo, who in his teens had been made Bishop of Bayeux. Taking advantage of the king's absence, the Count of Boulogne, dissatisfied with his share of the spoil after the conquest, attempted a revolt in Dover. It is unclear whether the Dovorians or Eustace, the count, initiated this, but Eustace sailed across the Channel with a contingent of knights and attempted to take Dover Castle from the Normans. The soldiers of the garrison there had no difficulty in seeing him off, and he fled in ignominy back to Boulogne, with most of his knights. The rest threw themselves over the White Cliffs.

It is not easy to find anything charitable to say about Odo, who was made Earl of Kent. Contemporaries had the same problem, describing him as 'a ravening wolf', 'rapacious' and 'destitute of virtue'. He became a huge land-owner in Kent, holding over 180 manors in the county, on top of the twelve he had elsewhere, making him the richest tenant-in-chief in the kingdom. He acquired the lands by the simple technique of forcibly seizing them and ejecting the English. As he was not only very rich but very powerful, being William's *de facto* regent during the latter's frequent stays in Normandy, resistance was not a wise choice.

The other major landowner in Kent was the Church, personified in Kent by the Archbishop of Canterbury. William had removed the shady Stigand in 1070, and replaced him with one of the Norman bishops, Lanfranc. The new archbishop resented Odo's expansionism, and their rivalry ended in 'The Trial of Penenden Heath', a three-day hearing before the nobles of the county which ended in Odo having to cede some of his lands to the Church.

Odo's subsequent fall and disgrace in 1082 are something of a mystery. He had planned a military expedition to Italy, possibly with the purpose of either seizing or buying the papacy. Whatever his plans, they displeased William, who imprisoned him and stripped him of his earldom. He was released in 1087 when William was dying.

William did not intend to make an empire of his new conquests, and on his death divided his territory in two: his son William Rufus got England and his oldest son, Robert, became Duke of Normandy. A year later, Odo, fresh out of gaol, was raising a revolt in Kent against William Rufus in favour of Robert. The rebellion lasted about six months, resulted in the burning of

Tonbridge and ended in the siege of Rochester Castle, in which Odo was captured. This time he was stripped of all his possessions and permanently exiled to Normandy.

The reign of William Rufus was short and he was succeeded by his younger brother, Henry I, who with indecent haste had himself crowned within three days. He was taking advantage of the fact that their older brother, Robert, who also wanted the throne, was away on a crusade. Robert tried the next year to invade England, but lost and Henry imprisoned him and took his dukedom, too.

Henry had a prodigious number of illegitimate children, but left only one legitimate heir, a daughter, Matilda, who as a woman was regarded unfavourably by some of the nobles of the country and whose claim to the throne was challenged by her cousin Stephen. Although Dover and Canterbury refused to admit him as king, London threw open its gates. The resultant civil war was ended by the deaths of both parties and the succession of Matilda's son Henry II in 1154. The first of the quarrelsome Plantagenets, he ruled, energetically and sometimes ruthlessly, for over thirty years and it was he who inadvertently turned Canterbury into one of the greatest pilgrimage sites in Christendom.

The importance of these monarchs for Kent rests in three great legacies: the Domesday Book, churches and castles.

William I had conquered England because it was a great prize and would bring him riches to continue his armed confrontations with his continental neighbours, with whom he was at almost permanent loggerheads. He also needed to reward his nobles for their ongoing support. He divided most of the land in England between these supporters soon after the conquest, and although he knew that he, and they, were now rich, he wanted to know exactly how rich and who had what.

The Domesday Book was commissioned at Christmas 1085 and a first draft was available for William before he left England forever at the end of the next year. (He died during his stay in Normandy while fighting yet another military campaign.) The book was an extraordinary achievement. The king and his successors would know what land he had, and who held it – under feudal law, the king was the owner of it all. It listed ploughlands, woodlands and meadows, and capital equipment such as ploughs or mills, and the overall value of each and provided a convenient reference point for

The Domesday Book entry for Sandwich. It says: *Sandwich lies in its own Hundred. The Archbishop holds this Borough. It is for the clothing of the monks. It pays the same service to the King as Dover* [i.e. ship service]. *The men of this Borough testify that before King Edward gave it to Holy Trinity, it paid £15 to the King. In 1066 it was not in the revenue. When the Archbishop acquired it, it paid £40 in revenue, and 40,000 herrings for the supplies of the monks. In the year in which this Survey was made Sandwich paid £50 in revenue and herrings as before. Before 1066 there were 307 habitable dwellings; now there are 76 more, that is 383 altogether.* (Professor John Palmer and George Slater, Open Domesday.org)

taxation purposes and in land dispute cases. It was carefully arranged by counties, themselves a Norman invention, and then by landholders within counties, all numbered consecutively for easy reference.

The Domesday Book starts with Kent – spelt Chenthe – on the very first page and the first town in the kingdom to be listed is Dover. It is among the 377 places in Kent which were visited by the assessors, ranging from populous towns like Canterbury to tiny settlements like Stowting and Barfrestone, which had only one household each.

Sandwich, owned by the Church, was clearly a thriving fishing town and port. The Church used the revenues it gained from the town for feeding and clothing the monks of the Cathedral Priory of the Holy Trinity in Canterbury, a Benedictine house.

The Domesday Book was not intended to be a census, but it does offer some clues as to how many people lived in the county. The total figure for Kent has been reckoned to be about 70–75,000. The most heavily populated areas were in the north-east, in a strip running westward from Folkestone, and in the Medway Valley. The Isle of Sheppey and the Weald were the least populated. The figures for towns are less reliable, but, very roughly, it seems that Canterbury, the largest town, had about 6,000 residents, Rochester, Dover and Sandwich 2,000–2,500 each and the flourishing Hythe and New Romney had 1,500-odd inhabitants between them. Hythe and New Romney are now quiet little backwaters. Maidstone, on the other hand, now the busy county town of Kent, had only fifty-seven villagers, a church, six mills, two salt-houses and a few fish ponds.

The Domesday Book shows that private land control in Kent was shared between three powerful men: Odo, who had the lion's share, Hugh de Montfort, with a largish lordship in the south-east, and Richard FitzGilbert, who held land around Tonbridge. The substantial royal manors at Faversham, Dartford, Milton Regis and Aylesford were under the direct control of the king, but a good half of the land in Kent was in the hands of the Church. On Odo's final disgrace in 1088, much of his land was taken back into royal hands, while some stayed with his sub-tenants. This meant that the Church became the single biggest landholder in the county.

The Church was expanding in all sorts of ways, starting at the centre, Canterbury. The new archbishop, Lanfranc, was about 65 years old when he was appointed in 1070, but still a forceful and inspiring leader who could not have been more different from his predecessor. A Benedictine monk of great learning and international repute, his great aim was to free the Church from the fetters of corruption. He transformed the Church in England and also his own church, Canterbury Cathedral.

The remains of Augustine's original cathedral building lie somewhere beneath the present cathedral's nave. It had been built across an old Roman road, and was a simple building consisting of a nave with side-chapels. During the ninth or tenth century this church was replaced by a larger structure which in turn was badly damaged by the Viking raid of 1011, and then mysteriously burnt to the ground in 1067. Lanfranc cleared the ruins and built a completely new cathedral to a design based closely on the abbey of St Etienne in Caen, his former bishopric, using stone brought over from France. This was a cruciform church, with an aisled nave of nine bays, a pair of towers at the west end, transepts with apses, and a low central tower with a steeple, crowned with a golden angel. It was dedicated in 1077, and not only glorified Christ but sent a clear message that the Normans were here to stay and that Norman architecture now ruled supreme. To hammer the message home, Lanfranc's right-hand man, another Benedictine called Gundulf, was created Bishop of Rochester, and built there his own imposing, and very Norman, cathedral.

A Benedictine abbey, Christ Church priory, had been added to Canterbury Cathedral in the tenth century, and Lanfranc added new cloisters, together with a chapter house, dormitory, refectory and cellar. He also built himself a splendid new palace, demolishing twenty-seven houses to make room for the building and its grounds in the city centre.

It is significant that he chose to live outside the abbey of which he was the head. Lanfranc was the first archbishop to regard himself as first and foremost an administrator of the Church rather than a priest or monk. He retained the nominal title of abbot but provided himself with a separate residence and revenues for the maintenance of his office of archbishop. To further enhance the post and its influence, he secured the primacy of the see of Canterbury over that of York. Canterbury now controlled every see in England, and Lanfranc's reforms led to the rebuilding and Normanisation of every existing Anglo-Saxon cathedral in the country.

The renovation of Canterbury Cathedral did not stop with Lanfranc's death. Over the next hundred years it was doubled in size, and ornately decorated. William of Malmesbury wrote of it: 'Nothing like it could be seen in England either for the light of its glass windows, the gleaming of its marble pavements or the many-coloured paintings which led the eyes to the panelled ceiling above.'

The rebuilding of Canterbury and Rochester cathedrals signalled the start of an unprecedented building programme in Kent. Churches were enlarged, or wholly rebuilt. Aisles and chapels were added and chancels enlarged. Windows were replaced. Towers were added, as a part of the plan (St Margaret-at-Cliff) or as an addition (New Romney).

The earliest post-Conquest churches were simple affairs, with a rectangular nave to the west and a smaller, square chancel to the east. Usually there was an archway between the two. Each part had a pitched roof running lengthways, thatched or covered with wooden shingles. Floors were of rammed earth, and interiors were painted to provide light and colour, to depict bible stories for the illiterate and to provide a horrible warning of what awaited the unrepentant sinner in hell. Sometimes side aisles were added, maybe to provide space for more altars or for extra processional space. Towers were especially expensive to build and indicative of a rich parish. Sandwich had no fewer than three churches with towers, reflecting its position as an important and growing town and port.

As part of his ambitious building programme, Lanfranc also set about establishing the first hospitals in England. These were to care for the poor,

St Mary's church, Brabourne, built in 1144 to replace a Saxon church, in typical Norman style, with a squat tower and rounded arches. One of its windows still has its original stained glass, the oldest in the country to do so. (Anne Thompson)

travellers, and pilgrims as well as the sick. The hospital of St John the Baptist in Canterbury was founded in 1085 for thirty men and thirty women, and just before his death Lanfranc founded another hospital, St Nicholas's, at Harbledown near Canterbury, the first in the country for lepers. Both these establishments still survive as almshouses. Not to be outdone, Gundulf of Rochester established his own hospital of St Bartholomew, for the leprous and poor, just outside the city. The siting of these lazar houses outside the walls of cities became the norm, although they were generally near main roads so that the afflicted inmates could beg for alms from passing travellers and pilgrims.

The trend for hospitals caught on, and they were built across the county in the ensuing couple of centuries, especially at the Channel ports and in settlements close to Watling Street, the road from Dover to London via Canterbury. Many subsequently became almshouses which offered permanent accommodation to the needy.

Those hospitals which offered beds to passing pilgrims received a huge trade boost in 1170 when Thomas Becket, the Archbishop of Canterbury, was murdered in his own cathedral. The four knights who committed the act had wrongly taken some ill-chosen and over-hasty words of Henry II about Becket, who was a thorn in his side, as a royal command to kill him.

The vile deed created a howl of anguish which was heard as far away as Rome, and the king was obliged by the Pope to carry out a suitably abject penance. He walked barefoot and in sackcloth from St Dunstan's church in Canterbury to the cathedral, where he was scourged by the monks, then spent the night in prayer, kneeling on the dirt floor. Becket, meanwhile, was elevated to the pantheon of the saints. The miracles started very soon after his death, and usually involved his blood, which had been conveniently collected at the site of the murder. Cloths soaked in this proved capable

The Hospital of St Stephen and St Thomas at New Romney was built in the twelfth century for the care of lepers, but by the fourteenth century had run out of sufferers and became a chantry. (Anne Thompson)

of curing the incurable and as time went on, prayers to Becket to inter-cede with the Almighty also produced results: sight was restored, leprosy cured and the lame walked. In the light of such incontrovertible evidence, canonisation was inevitable, and Becket was declared a saint in 1173, just twenty-six months after his martyrdom.

Henry, as shrewd a politician as ever graced the English throne, sensed the mood of the country and exploited it. His penance had been performed with maximum exposure and theatricality, and now, rather than shun-ning Thomas's cult, he embraced it. After every trip abroad, his first visit on English soil was to the saintly tomb, and he commissioned from the Canterbury monks a sumptuous Book of Miracles attributed to Thomas.

These miracles, and the king's patronage, led to fame, which led to pilgrim-ages. It was boom time in Canterbury, and to a lesser extent elsewhere in Kent. Canterbury hospitals accommodated the pilgrims who came from every part of England and the continent and crowded the city and cathedral. Then there were hospitals outside the city, like those at Ospringe and Dover, which catered only for Canterbury-bound pilgrims. Inns benefitted from the pil-grims who could afford their hospitality, and even brigands and highwaymen profited from unwary and, if Chaucer is to be believed, sometimes inebriated travellers. Shooters Hill on Watling Street was an infamous criminal haunt; another was Blean Woods, which get a mention in *The Canterbury Tales*.

There were other holy sites in Kent, and those near the arterial Watling Street were especially well-placed to attract pilgrims. At Newington, near Sittingbourne, a cross was erected to mark a stop Becket had made on his way to London not long before his death. Within a few years of the mar-tyrdom, it developed miraculous powers of its own and became a minor pilgrimage site. Thirty years after Becket's death, Rochester acquired its own martyr, William of Perth, a Scottish pilgrim, murdered by his own foster son while on his holy mission. His cult attracted thousands of visi-tors, especially after Edward I and his queen, Phillippa, visited his shrine.

Edward I, the great-grandson of Henry II, often stayed in Kent, at Leeds Castle which he had received as a coronation present, and with which, like everyone else who sees it, he had fallen in love. Although it is called a castle, it was never intended for military use and was really a fortified residence, built by a Norman noble in 1119 on the site of a wooden Saxon fortification.

Other Norman castles in Kent were built with very specific military purposes in mind. William the Conqueror had started castle building almost as soon as the Battle of Hastings was won. His 'shock and awe' tactics were successful, but the reality was that he had a tiny army, and he needed defensive structures to which he could retreat if it all went horribly wrong. He immediately built simple forts at Hastings and Pevensey, and then at Dover spent some time ensuring that the cliff-top fortifications met his requirements – they were certainly strong enough to repel the Count of Boulogne the following year. Later castles were built along the main lines of communication, to be used for national defence, such as those at Canterbury and Rochester.

None of these at first were the massive edifices they later became, but were simple motte-and-bailey forts. The bailey was a deep ditch surrounding a wooden palisade within which were accommodation and storage buildings. Inside the bailey, or sometimes next to it, was the motte, a hillock, made out of the spoil of the ditch on which was built a wooden fort. This had only one, easily defended, entrance, and was the place of final retreat in case of attack. They were cheap, easy to build and effective, but very susceptible to fire.

Once the Normans had established control, the forts were converted into the stone castles familiar to visitors today. The wooden motte was replaced with a fire-resistant stone hall or tower – the keep or, as it was then known, the *donjon*. This was then surrounded by stout stone walls, infilled with rubble, and the palisade walls of the baileys were also rebuilt in stone.

Castles were built to withstand sieges, if necessary, and to fend off attackers. They had battlements (or crenellations to give them their proper title) through which missiles could be hurled at attackers. Machicolations, a sort of overhanging structure with holes in the floor, allowed attackers scaling the walls to be targeted. Portcullises protected internal passageways. The gatehouse often had two, one at each end of the passageway: invaders would be trapped between them and the defenders in the room above would destroy them by firing arrows though murder-holes (*meurtrieres*) in the floor. The Normans did not use boiling oil. If they had any oil at all, they would have used it for cooking or lighting. Another interpretation of the existence of these holes is that water poured through them would quench fire in the gatehouse. Possibly they served both functions.

Tonbridge Castle has some fine examples of murder-holes, and it is likely that they were well used. The castle had been built on a bend in the river Medway, to protect the river crossing, soon after the Conquest, but for the next two centuries it was often itself under attack.

Its first owners, the FitzGilberts and Clares, had an unerring instinct for backing the wrong horse. In 1088, they supported Odo's rebellion against William Rufus, with the result that the castle, and most of the town of Tonbridge with it, was burnt to the ground. During the civil war created by the rival claims of Matilda and Stephen, they backed Matilda against the more dominant Stephen, with a similar outcome. A couple of generations later, now in possession of a fine stone keep, they played a major role in a rebellion against King John who, although a disaster as monarch, was a fine military strategist. He had no trouble at all taking the castle. When John's son Henry III was on the throne, the Clares sided with the rebel Simon de Montfort. This time the king seized the castle from them and once again put the town to the torch. His son Edward I gave the castle back, and the Clares thereafter carefully avoided rebellions, insurrections and plots.

Canterbury Castle, on the other hand, had a much more peaceful existence. The raised site of the first motte-and-bailey fort made use of an existing hillock, which had been a Roman burial mound. It was later abandoned in favour of a site by the city walls, and fourteen houses were demolished to make way for the new building, which was

Dane John at Canterbury, the site of the original motte-and-bailey fortification. The name is said to be a corruption of the word *donjon*. (Anne Thompson)

huge. Nearly 24m tall, with walls 4m thick, it never had to stand up to the attacks for which it was designed and was mostly used as a gaol. Unloved and unwanted, it was allowed to collapse until now only part of the keep is still standing.

Like Canterbury, Rochester Castle was built away from its motte-and-bailey predecessor. Although started by Lanfranc's protégé, Gundulf, the master builder William of Corbeil built the massive keep, the tallest in England, which still dominates the castle today. It had a huge strategic importance in guarding the Medway estuary and the bridge which carried Watling Street over the river towards London. Unlike Canterbury, it saw some fierce action. The original motte-and-bailey was used by Odo to garrison some of his troops during his rebellion against William Rufus. William besieged the castle, whose troops were weakened by disease and apparently by a plague of flies. They succumbed without much of an effort and Odo was taken prisoner.

The troubled reign of King John saw the next siege at Rochester, when the king decided to discipline the nobles who had forced his hand over the signing of Magna Carta. Some of them holed up at Rochester, but John, camped outside, brought in massive stone-throwing engines that pounded the castle day and night. He also tried mining the castle. Neither worked, so John deployed his secret weapon: dead pigs. He sent for 'forty of the fattest pigs of the type least good for eating', placed the carcasses by the props where the great tower had been undermined and set them on fire. The tower collapsed into the tunnel. The besieged nobles and their troops ate their own horses rather than surrender, but were eventually beaten by starvation. The tower was rebuilt – but made round instead of square, reflecting new trends in castle building learned during the crusades. Round towers could better deflect missiles and battering rams and were harder to scale.

The third siege of Rochester saw the king's men in the castle and the unruly barons outside. Henry III's troops were surrounded by the men of Simon de Montfort, the rebel leader, and it seemed that the barons had the upper hand. The day was saved when the king himself arrived with reinforcements and the besiegers fled. With them went the last of Rochester Castle's historical significance, and, like Canterbury, it was allowed to fall into disrepair.

Rochester Castle, on the east bank of the River Medway, now saved from dereliction and open to the public. (Anne Thompson)

Henry II's keep at Dover Castle is enormous, over 25 metres high with solid walls up to 6 metres thick. (Anne Thompson)

There was no military action at Hever and Leeds castles and both are better described as fortified houses, although they started life as motte-and-bailey compounds. Hever's claim to fame is that it was the birthplace of Anne Boleyn, but it was at Leeds Castle that Henry VIII lavished huge sums of money on creating a palace fit for a queen – his first wife, Catherine of Aragon. Saltwood Castle, near Hythe, has no known connection with the royal romance, but it was the overnight stop for three of the four murderous knights who the next day, 29 December 1170, went to Canterbury to confront Thomas Becket.

It is Dover Castle, however, which was and remains the greatest of them all. There were fortifications on the site above the town in Saxon times, and it was these that William the Conqueror adapted to his own specifications on his brief stay there in 1066. He, and his heirs, must have been satisfied that they were adequate, as no further work was done there for a hundred years. It was Henry II who in about 1180 started the great stone castle, bigger and more expensive than any so far built in England. Under the direction of Maurice the Engineer the great rectangular keep and the inner and outer bailies were built.

Henry's son Richard I spent more money on improving the castle, and his brother and successor John completed the outer walls and provided a new gatehouse. It now had every refinement of the up-to-date defence system: machicolations, arrow slits, crenellations, portcullises and murder-holes.

But it was not just a military construction. It was designed to provide sumptuous accommodation for the constable of the castle and for any visiting dignitaries from the continent. It has been suggested that this is one of the reasons that Henry II started the work, to impress foreign royalty en route to the tomb of the saint at Canterbury.

One of the first constables to live in this luxurious setting was King John's castellan Hubert de Burgh, a talented soldier, administrator and intellectual. In 1216, the castle was besieged by the heir to the French throne, Prince Louis, who had been invited by some disgruntled English barons to seize King John's crown. De Burgh was loyal to John, and with only 150 knights withstood a large French army, equipped with fearsome siege engines which hurled huge rocks at the castle, destroying one of its walls. He adopted the ingenious technique of tunnelling *out* of the castle in order

CONSTABLE'S TOWER, DOVER CASTLE

The constable's tower at Dover Castle was built to replace the northern gateway, breached in the siege of 1216. It consists of five conjoined towers standing well forward of the curtain wall. At the back is accommodation for the constable and his household. (Author's collection)

to mount surprise attacks on the French. The siege lost its *raison d'etre* when John died and was succeeded by his infant son Henry III. Louis still liked the idea of the English crown, however, and his fleet returned the next year, to be met off the coast of Sandwich by de Burgh and his much smaller outfit. De Burgh's knowledge of local conditions won him the day, and after the capture of their flagship and execution of its captain, the French beat a retreat, and Louis entered into peace negotiations.

De Burgh's successes won him the title of Earl of Kent, the position of regent to the young king, and marriage to Princess Margaret, sister of the King of Scotland. He found time during this busy career to found the Maison Dieu in Dover, a hospital originally for Canterbury-bound pilgrims, which the grateful Henry III visited when its chapel was consecrated. It is still in use today as the Town Hall.

The castle has remained an important royal fortress, becoming the seat of the Lord Warden of the Cinque Ports, and being extensively rebuilt during the Napoleonic Wars, when it also housed French prisoners of war. The entire site today occupies more than 141,000 square metres.

During the First World War, it served as a fire command post, and as a military command centre and hospital during the Second World War. During the subsequent Cold War its underground tunnels, where the rescue mission to Dunkirk had been planned, were designated as a shelter for the Regional Seat of Government in the event of a nuclear attack. The site was chosen for these roles as much for its symbolic status as for its strategic position.

Just before the Battle of Sandwich, in 1217, one of the uncles of the infant Henry III came to Dover Castle to propose that he should take it over on behalf of the French, as the king was too young to rule. De Burgh replied to him in words that have defined the castle ever since: 'Never will I yield to French aliens this castle, which is the very Key and Gate of England.'

Dover Castle has helped ensure that the men and women of Kent, and of England, can describe themselves as 'undefeated' for almost 1,000 years.

Three

WAR, PLAGUE AND REBELLION

The child king Henry III went on to rule for fifty-six years. When he succeeded to the throne in 1216, aged only 9 years, the authority and reputation of the monarchy were in tatters and constantly threatened by uprising and rebellion. Henry managed to placate his unruly barons early in his reign, but his expensive, and mostly disastrous, foreign policy lost him their trust. His father John, not called 'Lackland' for nothing, had lost the Crown's territory in Poitou, and Henry, determined to get it back, only succeeded in wasting a lot of money and a lot of lives. He squandered even more of the country's wealth on a futile attempt to put his son on the throne of Sicily, and borrowed substantial sums from the Pope.

Henry had started the practice of gathering together meetings of representatives from the court and the counties – gatherings called, for the first time in English history, parliaments. Their purpose was to agree taxes for the king's business. By the time of the Sicilian fiasco, they were refusing to agree to more taxation and the Pope was asking for his money back. Henry responded by extorting money from the senior clergy, who were forced to promise to pay unlimited sums towards the king's schemes, giving him effectively a blank cheque.

In 1258, exasperated by the king's profligacy, a group of barons seized control of the country. For five years the balance of power swung between king and rebels, until in 1263 the most radical of the insurgents, Simon de Montfort, staged a personal coup d'état. A vicious civil war followed, ending in de Montfort's defeat, death and horrible mutilation at the Battle of Evesham in 1265.

The Cinque Ports played an important role at critical points of Henry's reign. The English ships at the Battle of Sandwich, which saved the throne of England for young Henry, were supplied by the Cinque Ports; they came to the rescue with men and ships when the Poitou campaign resulted in naval battles in the Bay of Biscay. Henry then ordered them to harass and plunder the coastal towns of France, a task they undertook with enthusiasm. The king took a fifth of the proceeds and the Ports came to be known as 'the king's pirates'. In 1263, however, they turned their backs on Henry and sided with de Montfort. Twenty-eight Portsmen attended the parliament he called, and, appreciative of their support, he gave them the proceeds of a tax on the clergy to rebuild their ships.

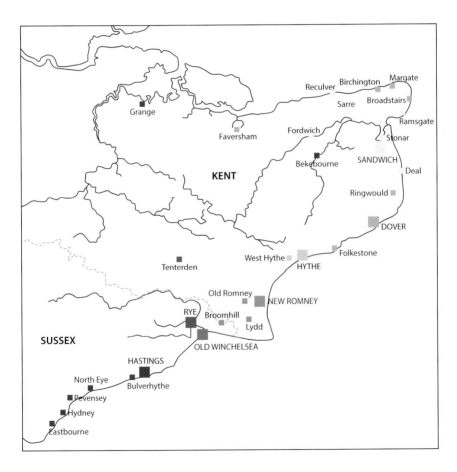

The five original Cinque Ports and their limbs.

The Ports were by then far more in number than the five named in the Domesday Book. Although the name 'Cinque Ports' is not used in the survey, the growing fishing towns of Dover, Hythe, Sandwich and Romney (and Hastings, in Sussex) paid the king 'sea service' and as compensation received 'dues and fines' which normally would have gone to the king. All the ports gradually acquired an accretion of their own limbs, so that by the mid-twelfth century no fewer than forty-two ports, towns and villages comprised the powerful Confederation of the Cinque Ports in Kent and Sussex.

'Sea service' meant supplying ships to the king for fifteen days a year, free of charge, to carry out his orders. This could be repelling raids on the coast, naval service as part of a larger royal fleet, or, more peaceably, transporting the king and his household to and from the continent. The rewards were generous: tax exemption, self-government, permission to raise taxes and to punish criminals, and entitlement to wreck salvage. Each port provided its quota of ships. Dover, for example, had to provide nineteen, Hythe five, Romney four and Bekesbourne, one. The inclusion of Bekesbourne, a small, landlocked village south of Canterbury, in the Confederation is unexpected but has its rationale. The family which owned the manor of Hastings also owned Bekesbourne, which accordingly became a 'limb' of the port. Its solitary ship was a significant one: berthed at Hastings, it was the king's personal ferry, a sort of medieval Royal Yacht.

During the relatively peaceful years of the twelfth century, the Cinque Ports operated more or less as a cross-Channel ferry service for the king, his family and entourage, bore the canopy over the sovereign at coronations, another of their rights, and carried on fishing. It was fishing that led them to start flexing their combined muscles.

By the time of their success at the Battle of Sandwich in 1217, the Portsmen were flocking to the annual Yarmouth herring fair to take advantage of the abundant and very lucrative catch. In 1215, King John had given the Ports the right to administer their own justice to fellow-Portsmen while in Yarmouth. Unsurprisingly, the citizens of Yarmouth were less than enthusiastic about this encroachment on their authority, and relations between them and the Cinque Ports were often fractious, if not violent. In 1277, Edward I, the son of Henry III, extended the Cinque Ports' authority at the fair, which so incensed the Yarmouth men that the event often turned into a rowdy free-for-all.

The nadir was reached when, in 1297, the Yarmouth and Cinque Ports contingents of a royal fleet set to fighting each other instead of the enemy. Twenty Yarmouth ships were burnt and their crews with them. In subsequent musters, the two factions were kept well apart, although the hostilities rumbled on in the form of petty acts of vindictiveness for centuries. As late as the seventeenth century the Yarmouth men refused for days to acknowledge the presence of the Cinque Ports men in their town, because the latter had not doffed their hats for long enough at the start of proceedings.

The post of Lord Warden of the Cinque Ports was created to ensure cohesion between the Ports, and, because it was combined with the position of Constable of Dover Castle, the postholder became responsible for the defence of the whole of the vulnerable Kent and Sussex coasts. He also had the powers of an admiral in the ports: he held inquests on wrecks, issued licences for cross-Channel passage, supervised customs operations and took action against anyone who blocked ports, and received a healthy share of wreck salvage. It was a powerful, and very lucrative, post.

The Ports became rich, too, from wreck salvage, from war plunder – and from piracy. Piracy was not legal and not officially sanctioned, but a blind eye was turned because the Ports were useful to the king and his defence of the realm. Piracy happened as and when the opportunity arose. In 1235, when England and France were at peace, the Cinque Ports ships seized and plundered French merchant ships, tearing up their letters of safe conduct and throwing their crews overboard to drown. At Sandwich, a major importer of wine and luxury foodstuffs, the Portsmen could not resist the temptation to enrich themselves even further by pilfering the cargoes of the Venetian galleys which used the town as a staging post. Even Edward I, a strong, sometimes brutal king, was in thrall to the Ports, which supported his campaigns against the Welsh in 1278 and 1282, and against Scotland in 1290. In 1299 they were self-assured enough to tell him that if he threatened their liberties they would turn to piracy full-time, and 'make their profit wheresoever they could find it'.

They did not know it, but by then the tide of their fortunes had begun to turn. The great storm of 1287 had silted up harbours, blocked and diverted rivers, and submerged towns. For the time being, they were able to overcome these setbacks, but the glory days were almost over.

The new century saw a new monarch. Edward I was succeeded by his son Edward II in 1307. A year later the ships of the Cinque Ports carried him to France to marry the French Princess Isabella, and in 1325, they carried her back there, ostensibly on a diplomatic mission. Isabella, though, had plans of her own and while in France joined forces with the king's enemy, the exiled Roger Mortimer. The pair invaded England the following year and sought to depose the king and replace him with his son. The Cinque Ports supported Mortimer and Isabella, and took part in a deputation to Edward to persuade him to abdicate. When he did not, he was deposed anyway and imprisoned in Berkeley Castle, where he died. Mortimer himself only lasted another three years before being overthrown by the young man he had put on the throne, Edward III.

This Edward's favourite pursuit was the art of war. In 1337, already at war with Scotland, he retaliated against Scotland's ally France, who had been raiding ports on the south coast, including Dover, Folkestone and Sandwich. This marked the beginning of the Hundred Years War. It was not continuous, though it must have seemed like it to those who lived on the Kent coast.

The Cinque Ports rallied to the call to arms and provided ships for one of the first naval engagements of the war, the Battle of Sluys in 1340, and they were there at the siege of Calais six years later. As the war dragged on, large-scale naval engagements were replaced by hit-and-run raids on both sides of the Channel and the declining importance of the Ports became obvious. Their little merchant ships, the cogs, of 30 to 60 tons, crewed by twenty-odd men, fell out of favour. The king wanted bigger, faster ships, such as those provided by Yarmouth, Southampton, Poole and Portsmouth. The Ports' havens and harbours were silting up, and the Venetian galleys abandoned Sandwich for Southampton. The Ports were still useful to the war effort, though: in 1354 all their carpenters and shipwrights were forcibly mustered and set to work on the king's ships. It was a long way from the days of unchecked piracy on the high seas and blackmailing the King of England.

But they remained, as long as their harbours and havens stayed open, important ports of arrival and departure, and they retained, and continued for hundreds of years to retain, their privileges and rights. One of the most sought-after of their honours was the right to carry the canopy over the monarch at the coronation, and to join him or her afterwards at the ceremonial banquet. The tradition lasted until 1821. There was competition within the ports for the role, but the selection was always of tall, reasonably presentable men who had deep pockets – the elaborate silk and satin scarlet robes did not come cheap. There were compensations, however. The silver staves which supported the canopy were afterwards broken up and divided among the canopy bearers to take home, to be melted down and sold or turned into keepsakes.

The Hundred Years War rumbled on. Edward III's heir apparent, the Black Prince, a great and (usually) chivalric warrior, covered himself in glory at Crecy in 1346, in Poitiers, where he captured the French king, and in Limoges, but succumbed to a mystery illness which killed him in 1376, aged 45. Lying on his deathbed, he asked for water from a well at Harbledown near Canterbury which had previously cured him, and at his request he was buried in Canterbury Cathedral, next to the shrine of Thomas Becket. His 'achievements', or hatchments, of helmet, gauntlets, quilted surcoat, shield and scabbard are still displayed near his magnificent tomb.

Seven years later it was the Black Prince's son, Richard, who succeeded Edward to the throne of England as Richard II. Richard made some attempts to secure a negotiated and final peace with France, but his narcissism, insistence on the majesty of his own person and unshakeable belief in the royal prerogative did not endear him to many, and he was deposed in 1399 by his cousin, Henry Bolingbroke.

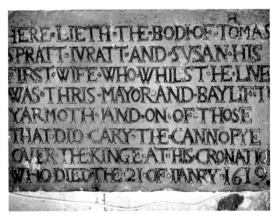

Thomas Spratt of Hythe was chosen to carry the canopy at the coronation of James I of England. He was by trade a draper, so presumably could buy the expensive cloth for his outfit at wholesale prices. (St Leonard's church, Hythe)

The Black Prince's Well at Harbledown, which bears his coat of arms of three feathers. Although its water failed to cure the prince, its healing properties continued to attract visitors until the nineteenth century. (Author's collection)

As Henry IV, the first Lancastrian king, he spent most of his fourteen-year reign defending himself against plots, rebellions and assassination attempts. His son, Henry V, made war with France a personal project, won the Battle of Agincourt and forced the French to sign a peace treaty. All his work was undone during the reign of his son, Henry VI. By the 1450s, the only remaining English territory in France was Calais, but at last, the war was over.

The Hundred Years War was fought mostly at sea and overseas, and impacted very little on the people of inland England. Kent, with its long coastline, suffered more, and French raids inflicted terrible damage. The fear of incursions in the county led to another round of castle building.

Westenhanger Castle, near Hythe, was built as a response to invasion fears in 1343. Constructed with massive towers, it was not called upon to defend the realm during the Hundred Years War, but was used by Elizabeth I as her command centre for the troops gathered to defend the country against the Spanish Armada in 1588. It is barely a stone's throw away from Lympne Castle, extensively rebuilt and fortified during the same period.

At Cooling, between Rochester and Gravesend, the owners got the permission of Richard II to improve their fortifications after a series of damaging French raids in the Thames estuary in 1378. Warfare was changing and Cooling Castle was the first in England to reflect this. Its builders installed ten 3ft-long holes in the walls for arquebuses. The arquebus was an early muzzle-loading firearm, its great advantage being that at close range it could pierce steel-plate armour. The effectiveness of the weapon was never tested at Cooling, as the only time the castle saw action was not against the French, but when Sir Thomas Wyatt besieged it during his 1554 rebellion against Queen Mary. Under attack by two cannons, it lasted exactly eight hours and was so badly damaged it had to be abandoned.

French raids on the Cinque Ports of Rye, Hastings and Winchelsea at around the same time prompted the building of Scotney Castle just on the Kent side of the border with Sussex. It is ideally placed for defensive purposes on an island in the middle of a lake, which can only be approached via another island. Two hundred years after it was built it was no longer defensible, but became instead the sanctuary of fugitive Roman Catholic priests during the sixteenth and seventeenth centuries.

On one of the towers of the gatehouse of Cooling Castle is the following inscription: Knouwyth that beth and schul be/That I am mad in help of the cuntre/In knowing of whyche thing/Thys is chartre and wytnessyng. The gist is that the castle is there to protect the people, not built against them. (Anne Thompson)

The last royal castle of the medieval period was erected on the Isle of Sheppey between 1361 and 1377, although whether as a defensive structure or as a bolt-hole for the royal family is a moot point. A whole town sprang up around the building and was named Queenborough in honour of Edward II's wife. In 1388 it was declared a royal borough. Queenborough is still there, but the castle is long gone, its only claim to any military fame being to repel a rather half-hearted attack by Jack Cade and his rabble of rebellious Kent men in 1450. The town became an important port for the export of wool, and was briefly a Wool Staple, one of only two places in Kent through which all wool for export was compulsorily directed.

Wool was one of England's main exports during the thirteenth and fourteenth centuries, sold to be spun and woven in the Low Countries. At the peak of the trade, in the early fourteenth century, about 40,000 sacks were sent abroad each year, the fleeces from 10 million sheep. Some of the finest came from the Romney Marsh, where the newly reclaimed land was largely owned and managed by Christ Church priory in Canterbury.

From 1331, the wool also fed a developing domestic cloth industry in Cranbrook, which reached its peak towards the end of the Tudor period. Edward III wanted to break the monopoly in broadcloth manufacture enjoyed by the Netherlands. He poached Flemish weavers, fullers and dyers by offering incentives and protection. Cranbrook, with streams to drive mills, oak timber to build them with, and deposits of fuller's earth to finish the cloth, was an ideal location for the new craftsmen and women. The popularity of the town's speciality, a broadcloth called Cranbrook Gray, led to prosperity and, like most prosperous medieval towns, Cranbrook displayed its wealth in its church. Successive extensions to the building were made over the years, creating eventually the vast 'Cathedral of the Weald' which now dominates a peaceful little country town of weatherboarded houses.

The export of cloth became a new success story for England, which was, in the middle of the fourteenth century, enjoying considerable prosperity under the reign of Edward III. The Scots had been trounced, and so, temporarily, had the French. The country was rich, and the wealth of its aristocracy trickled down to merchants, tradesmen and small farmers.

St Dunstan's Church Cranbrook. Its 22.5-meter-high tower, completed in 1425, contains the prototype for the Big Ben clock in London. (Anne Thompson)

But two years after the Black Prince's triumph at Crecy, and just as Cranbrook was starting to benefit from its cloth industry, a ship from Gascony landed at Melcombe in Dorset one summer's day. One of its crew brought with him bubonic plague. By October 1348 it was rife in Dorset, by March the next year it was in Devon and Cornwall and Norfolk, Suffolk, Surrey and Hampshire. By July it was spreading across the northern counties and by the end of the year nowhere in England had been spared. Over a period of roughly two years, perhaps a third of the population died.

The Black Death arrived in Kent not only from the West, but through the Channel ports from Europe. A monk of Rochester Cathedral recorded its effects there and tells of bereaved parents carrying their children to the plague pits and throwing their bodies in, without the benefit or comfort of a Christian burial. The Bishop of Rochester, Hamo of Hythe, then in his seventies, lost thirty-two members of his small household and retired to his country manor at Trottiscliffe where he bewailed his fate, and that of the country at large.

Conversely, the priory of Christ Church at Canterbury suffered little, and the stream of pilgrims to the shrine of Thomas Becket continued unabated. It is impossible to say whether these pilgrims were offering thanks for deliverance, or praying for it.

The epidemic did not bring out the best in people anywhere, and Kent was no exception. On his return from Trottiscliffe to Rochester, old Hamo found that his surviving clergy were holed up at home, or deserting their flocks rather than run the risk of infection by carrying out their priestly duties. Even in Canterbury, less badly affected, congregations were unable to receive the sacraments because their priests had run away to save their skins. Many contemporary reports say that the whole country fell into a sort of depraved hopelessness, that evil and sin were the legacy of the terrible visitation. In Kent, the monk of Rochester tells how every kind of vice was practised by the greater part of the population, clergy included, without a thought for their own salvation.

Dode church, which was deconsecrated in 1367 but restored in the nineteenth century. Today it is a wedding venue. (Anne Thompson)

The colossal death toll meant that fields were left unworked and livestock untended. Some villages were completely wiped out, or so badly depopulated that their remaining residents left. Dode, a hamlet in the North Downs of Kent, was one of these. Its church still stands on a mound at what would have been the centre of the settlement. Local legend has it that the last survivor of the Black Death, the Dodechild, a 7-year-old girl, took refuge in the church after all the other villagers were dead, and died within its walls. She is supposed to haunt the churchyard, appearing every seven years.

The depopulation caused by the Black Death meant that land became relatively plentiful and manpower in much shorter supply. Wages rose and the profits of landowners were eroded. Trading, commercial and financial networks crumbled. The authorities responded to the chaos with panic legislation and attempts to fix wages at pre-plague levels, making it a crime to refuse work and branding anyone who did. The royal government had not intervened in this way before, nor allied itself with local landowners quite so blatantly.

The government courted further unpopularity through taxation. The Hundred Years War was enormously expensive. By the 1370s, the garrisons in Calais and Brest alone cost £36,000 a year to maintain, and military expeditions could consume £50,000 in six months. Just before the death of Edward III, Parliament approved a new form of taxation, the poll tax, which was levied on everyone over the age of 14. The advisors of the new king, Richard II, managed to run through the £22,000 raised very quickly and returned to Parliament again and again for still larger sums. By November 1380, they wanted the colossal sum of £160,000 and a new, higher rate of poll tax was introduced. Many in Kent and the south-east in general tried to evade it by refusing to register for the tax. In March 1381, the royal council appointed commissioners to go out to the towns and villages, find the tax dodgers and exact payment.

On 30 May, one of these officials summoned some defaulting Essex villagers to Brentford to pay their debts. They refused, he had them arrested, and in the ensuing violence several townsmen were killed. By the next day, the revolt was spreading. On 4 June, some Essex protesters marched towards London, others to Kent, where a similar insurgency was flaring. A man accused of being an escaped serf had been imprisoned in Rochester Castle.

A furious crowd, demanding the right of every man to work where he chose, was led by the baker Robert Cave to Dartford and on to Maidstone. There they stormed the gaol, freed the radical preacher John Ball, and marched on to Rochester. The constable in charge of Rochester Castle surrendered it without a fight and freed the prisoner.

Some of the Kentish mob now continued under the leadership of John Ball and Wat Tyler, a local man, to Canterbury which they entered without resistance on 10 June. They created mayhem in the city and threw open the gaol before leaving to advance on London, armed with sticks, battle axes, old swords and bows.

Along their way, they encountered the king's mother, who was mocked but otherwise left unharmed. The Kentish rebels reached Blackheath, just south-east of the capital, on 12 June. There, John Ball, a 'hedge priest' with no parish, who had been imprisoned several times for his dissenting beliefs, addressed the men, famously asking 'When Adam delved and Eve span, who was then a gentleman?'

Ball and Tyler used the rebel slogan 'With King Richard and the true commons of England' to rally their men. They were loyal to the king, believing that he was advised by evil men and that they were his best counsellors. But while Tyler was negotiating with King Richard, a breakaway group took the Tower of London and beheaded the Archbishop of Canterbury, who was sheltering there. It was the beginning of the end. At Tyler's next encounter with the king, violence broke out between their respective supporters and Tyler was killed, his head placed on a pole and carried through the city to be displayed on London Bridge. John Ball was taken, and hanged, drawn and quartered in the presence of the 14-year-old Richard. The Kentish rebels went home, some of them to face execution themselves, but Parliament and the king quietly forgot about the poll tax, and in the twenty-first century it is Tyler and Ball who are celebrated, not their oppressors.

The ease with which the rebels had entered Canterbury, and the arbitrary execution of the archbishop gave its authorities pause for thought, and the city walls were repaired and strengthened and a new West Gate erected. The towers along the length of the wall incorporated modern gun-loops rather than arrow slits. So well built were they that 600 years later it is still

The county town of Maidstone has named a road after its famous son Wat Tyler – but both Dartford and Deptford claim him as theirs as well. (Anne Thompson)

possible to walk along the ramparts, and the West Gate, which replaced the castle as the city gaol, still straddles a main thoroughfare.

The Canterbury authorities had more building to do thirty years later when an earthquake struck the city. The bell tower of the cathedral was damaged and the six bells were 'shook down'. The archbishop was presiding at a synod to examine the allegedly heretical beliefs of John Wycliffe when the earthquake struck. Wycliffe had inspired many of the teachings of John Ball. The meeting was suspended, and both parties claimed divine intervention on their behalf.

Seventy years after the Peasants' Revolt, another national rebellion started in Kent, when Jack Cade, who called himself 'Captain of Kent' gathered an army of disgruntled supporters at Ashford and marched towards London, demanding to present the king with their 'Complaint of the Poor Commons of Kent'. This uprising was caused more directly by the circumstances of the Hundred Years War.

The West Gate, Canterbury. The drum towers of this 18m-high western gate of the city wall form the largest surviving city gate in England. (Anne Thompson)

Towards the end of the war, in 1450, there was once again widespread fear of invasion. Kent and Sussex were seeing regular attacks by the French and Henry VI's order to set warning beacons along the coast confirmed their suspicions that a major onslaught was imminent. Ill-equipped and hungry, English soldiers were plundering towns in Kent on their way to and from Channel ports, and their victims had no recourse to compensation. To add to the volatile mix, many believed that the king had surrounded himself with corrupt advisors. The Duke of Suffolk, a favourite of the king who had sent him abroad to prevent his execution for treason, was found minus his head on the beach at Dover. Rumours began to circulate that the king was planning to avenge his friend's murder by turning the whole of the county into a royal forest.

About 5,000 men marched with Jack Cade in the spring of 1450. Their manifesto included a list of complaints and demands to be brought before the king. The rebels denied any complicity in the murder of the Duke of Suffolk; they called for enquires into corruption in government and for the removal of corrupt officials; they charged Henry with injustice for protecting traitors like Suffolk and accused his advisors of extortion and misuse of power. Names were named and included the most powerful men in the land as well as local magnates.

Hoping to put a lid on the rebellion before it got too heated, Henry sent a small armed contingent to deal with it. His men were led into an ambush at Sevenoaks, and in the skirmish their leaders were killed and their bodies stripped. The rebellion spread. On 29 June, the Bishop of Salisbury, the king's confessor and close advisor, was murdered by a mob in Wiltshire, and the king, seriously rattled, put some distance between himself and the rebels by retreating to Warwickshire. Cade took his rebels to London, where he declared himself mayor, and the subjects of his 'Complaint' were tried by kangaroo court and summarily executed.

The rebellion ended messily. Cade lost control of his men, who drank, raped and looted their way through London. The citizens retaliated, and after a pitched battle on London Bridge, Cade was persuaded that the king would meet his demands and pardon the rebels. This was, of course, retracted almost immediately once the rebels had laid down their arms. Cade was killed, and his body parts distributed across Kent as a dreadful warning to any other potential insurgents. His supporters were hunted down in Canterbury, Faversham, Rochester and the Isle of Sheppey and executed.

The weakness of Henry VI, who had passed the rebellion cowering in Kenilworth Castle, had been laid bare, and the mendacity of his advisors exposed. Cade's 'Complaint' had included the demand that the king restore the Duke of York as his advisor. York, who like Cade presented himself as an anti-corruption reformer, returned from Ireland (where he had conveniently been found long-term duties by the king) in the autumn of 1450. His campaign against the king continued until, in 1456 he imprisoned Henry, by then mentally unbalanced, and appointed himself Protector of England.

It was the start of the Wars of the Roses.

For decades the houses of Lancaster and York fought each other for the throne of England. The Lancastrian Henry VI was succeeded by the Duke of York's son, Edward IV. He in turn should have been succeeded by his young son, Edward V, but the boy's uncle, Richard of Gloucester, seized the throne, and young Edward and his brother disappeared from view into the Tower of London, later being declared dead. The wicked uncle was Richard III. Henry Tudor, a very distant Lancastrian relative, then defeated Richard at the Battle of Bosworth in 1485. He was crowned Henry VII, married Elizabeth of York, daughter of Edward IV, and succeeded in uniting and reconciling the two houses and ending the wars.

In the early stages of the war, Kent was Yorkist. The Duke of York seemed to fill the vacancy left by Jack Cade, and Kent had reason to be thankful to his supporter, the Duke of Warwick, as well. In 1457, Sandwich had been attacked by a large French force, resulting in the death of the mayor, among many others. (On ceremonial occasions, the Mayor of Sandwich still wears sombre black mourning in memory of this event.) Warwick was then Constable of Calais and, against the wishes of the Crown, went hell for leather against the offenders in what were, essentially, illegal acts of piracy. The people of Kent cared not whether the retribution was legal or not, and when Warwick landed in Sandwich in 1460 to support the Duke of York, they rose up in his support and marched with him to take London.

Warwick is known to history as 'The Kingmaker'. By 1469, having succeeded in putting the Duke of York's son on the throne, he was feeling aggrieved because the new king, Edward IV, was not grateful enough. He started plotting against him, and in July arrived in Kent, inviting anyone who would help him to present themselves fully armed at Canterbury on 16 July. He intended to reinstate Henty VI, who was in exile. The plea was successful. Four days later he left the city at the head of a substantial force to march on London. It seems that Kent supported Warwick, rather than whoever was on the throne at the time, York or Lancaster, but the coup d'etat failed.

The rest of the bloody battles that eventually led to Bosworth Field took place in the Midlands and North of England, leaving Kent in peace. After the death of Richard III on the battlefield and the accession of the first Tudor, Henry VII, there must have been a collective sigh of relief in Kent that at last peace had broken out.

Four

REFORMATION AND REVOLUTION

After the carnage of Bosworth, Henry VII had no appetite for war, and for some years the tranquillity of Kent remained undisturbed. He did have to deal with a few abortive attempts at rebellion early in his reign, including from a couple of Yorkist impersonators, Lambert Simnel and Perkin Warbeck. The latter, trading on his remarkable resemblance to Edward IV, persuaded some die-hard Yorkists that he was in fact Edward's younger son, Richard, who had not, after all, died in the Tower, but had been miraculously preserved and now wished to claim his rightful throne. He was supported by a Burgundian 'aunt', who had a personal grudge against Henry VII, and she funded Warbeck's military expedition to England. In 1495, he attempted to land at Deal, but after 150 of his troops had been killed without him even disembarking he went off to enlist the help of the Irish and Scots instead. Four years later he was captured, confessed and was hanged.

Henry's strategic marriage to Margaret of York produced the necessary heir and spare, and freed from serious invasion threats, the king settled down to looking at his balance sheets. He is not known to history as Henry the Accountant, but probably should be: he checked and signed every single entry in the Treasury account books. He had appointed John Morton as Archbishop of Canterbury early in his reign and soon afterwards made him Lord Chancellor and instructed him to replenish the royal coffers, which had been severely depleted by the Wars of the Roses. Morton's simple idea was that no one was to be exempted from taxes: 'If the subject is seen to live frugally, tell him because he is clearly a money saver of great ability, he can afford to give generously to the king. If, however, the subject lives a life of great extravagance, tell him he, too, can afford to give largely, the proof of his opulence being evident in his expenditure.' This, 'Morton's fork', worked exceptionally well and made Henry a rich man. Morton lived at Knole House, near Sevenoaks, where a young Thomas More acted as his page.

Henry died a rich man, and left the throne to the 'spare'. His elder son, Arthur, had died aged 15, and the younger son, Henry, succeeded as Henry VIII. Aged only 17, he had, a few days before his coronation, married Arthur's widow, Catherine of Aragon, after obtaining a papal dispensation to do so, and was rewarded almost immediately by a pregnancy. This, like all the others that Catherine endured, ended in disappointment.

Henry's connections with Kent had started when he was very young indeed. In 1493, at the age of only 3, he was appointed Lord Warden of the Cinque Ports and Constable of Dover Castle. The actual work associated with the roles was carried out by Sir Edward Poynings, who continued in the posts after Henry succeeded to the throne. Poynings lived at Westenhanger, where he rebuilt the by now dilapidated castle, eventually giving it to Henry, who laid out a deer park in its grounds.

Glamorous and ambitious, Henry VIII had little interest in accounts books but believed his destiny to be the emulation of Henry V, who had subdued France. He did manage, early in his reign, to capture a couple of insignificant French towns in a campaign organised by his closest advisor, Cardinal Wolsey, but his later military efforts, despite massive expenditure, were failures. It was also Wolsey who coordinated the extravagant display of the Field of the Cloth of Gold in 1520. Its aim was to develop a bond of friendship between the French and English monarchs, and while it may not have been entirely successful in that, it certainly allowed Henry and Francis I, his French counterpart, the opportunity to compete in sheer, no-holds barred ostentation.

The ostentation started before Henry had even left his own kingdom. He chose Leeds Castle in Kent as his jumping-off point. He had already spent considerable sums on transforming the castle into a palace for Queen Catherine and a statement of his own wealth. Glass, expensive and luxurious, was used extensively. Catherine's suite of rooms had fireplaces decorated with the royal arms and Spanish motifs, entwined with lovers' knots. New stables were built, and a new chapel for the pious queen. When Henry rode off to the coast to take the ships provided by the Cinque Ports to France, he took with him provisions from the Leeds larders and venison from its park for the feasts which would follow.

Six years later, Henry may have been regretting those love knots: he had fallen for another woman, Anne Boleyn, a daughter of Kent who had grown up at her father's home, Hever Castle.

Thomas Boleyn had inherited Hever and used it as a base from which to scrabble up the greasy pole of social advancement, using whatever means he could. His first, quite large, step up was achieved by marrying the daughter of Thomas Howard, later to be Duke of Norfolk. In 1501, the year of his daughter Anne's birth, he attended the wedding of Catherine of Aragon and Prince Arthur, and two years later accompanied Arthur's sister, Margaret, north for her wedding to the King of Scotland. When Henry VIII succeeded to the throne, Thomas Boleyn was sufficiently well known to the young king to be made a knight. He excelled at the pastimes that Henry loved – jousting, hawking, bowls – and became a fixture at court. He undertook some diplomatic missions in France for the king, and used his connections there to get his daughters, Mary and Anne, places at the French court.

When Thomas Boleyn died, Henry VIII took possession of Hever Castle and gave it to Anne of Cleves as part of her annulment settlement. (Author's collection)

On their return to England, both women were accepted at Henry's court. Mary, although married by this time, soon became Henry's mistress, and possibly the mother of his son. Her father was rewarded by being ennobled as Viscount Rochford in 1525. Having ditched Mary, Henry became enamoured of her sister Anne the next year, although she resisted his advances until she was certain that he would be free to marry her. His wooing was ardent and he often descended unannounced on Hever Castle to canoodle with his beloved. Henry's gifts to Anne during their protracted courtship were generous and included the promotion of both her father and her brother, George. Thomas became an earl, and later Lord Privy Seal. George was made a viscount and in 1534, by which time he was the king's brother-in-law, Lord Warden of the Cinque Ports.

In order to marry Anne, Henry needed to divest himself of Catherine, who had proved a disappointment in producing only a daughter, Mary. When Thomas Wolsey failed to get the Pope to agree to a divorce, Henry turned to another cleric for advice. Thomas Cranmer convinced him that the bible, not the Pope, was the infallible source of the truth. The 'Great Matter' of the king's divorce was no longer a private affair but began to be discussed openly among people of all stations of life. Anne had her supporters, but many more detractors. Among these was Elizabeth Barton, the Holy Maid of Kent.

Elizabeth was born in humble circumstances in Aldington, not far from Ashford, where she grew up and became a farm servant. In 1525, when she was about 18, she started to see visions and claimed to have received divine revelations predicting future events. She attracted considerable attention, and her concerned parish priest sought the advice of the Archbishop of Canterbury, William Warham. A commission appointed by him decided that she was indeed divinely guided and she took the veil as a Benedictine nun at St Sepulchre's Priory in Canterbury.

In 1528, she held a private meeting with Cardinal Wolsey and later with Henry himself. Their friendship soured, however, when Elizabeth began to prophesy that if Henry married Anne he would lose his throne within a month and that the kingdom would suffer from a great plague.

Irrespective of the Maid's warning, Henry and Anne married on 25 January 1533. She was pregnant with, Henry hoped, his longed-for male heir. Cranmer, whom Henry had made Archbishop of Canterbury after Warham's death, declared the marriage to Catherine void and the union with Anne valid. He crowned Anne queen and became godparent to the disappointing daughter, Elizabeth, that she produced later that year.

Henry, perhaps emboldened by finding himself ruling a plague-free kingdom well after his marriage, ordered the arrest of the Holy Maid of Kent. She confessed to Thomas Cromwell, Wolsey's successor as chief adviser to the king, that she was a fraud. It did not save her. She was hanged for treason at Tyburn, and her head put on a stake on London Bridge. She has the dubious distinction of being the only woman so dishonoured.

The king's marriage to Anne Boleyn was not a success. She also failed to produce a son, and barely three years after her wedding was executed on trumped-up charges of treason. These included incest with her brother George, who was beheaded two days before Anne. Old Thomas Boleyn was removed from his office as Lord Privy Seal and retired in disgrace to Hever, where he died and is buried.

The church of St Peter, Hever, burial place of Thomas Boleyn. (Anne Thompson)

One survivor of the crisis was the poet Thomas Wyatt, an early admirer of Anne's, imprisoned in the Tower with her brother but eventually cleared of treason and released back to his home, Allington Castle near Maidstone. 'These bloody days have broke my heart,' he told his father.

Encouraged by Cranmer and Cromwell, Henry set about severing his ties with the Church in Rome. The Pope was now, in Cranmer's words 'the Antichrist of the Apocalypse' and Henry, under the Act of Supremacy, became head of the Church in England. As such, he was also head of all the religious houses in England. The financial opportunities they presented to a cash-strapped monarch were attractive. He and Cromwell dispatched commissioners to visit every religious establishment in the country, ostensibly to find out how much they were worth for taxation purposes, but also to gather information, mostly scurrilous, about lapses in religious practice.

The gatehouse of Faversham Abbey, all that remains of the religious house founded in 1148 by King Stephen. He was buried there in 1154. (Anne Thompson)

This often gave enough reason for the houses to be closed and their income and property surrendered to the Crown.

By the end of 1535, the suppression of smaller houses had started and although Henry continued for a while to maintain piously that his sole objective was monastic reform, it became increasingly clear that official policy was now the extinction of monasticism in the country. By 1540, all the religious houses were gone, their lands, money and possessions transferred to the king to dispose of as he wished. He said he would use the money for the defence of the realm.

In Kent, seventeen monasteries, five nunneries and six friaries were liquidated. Langdon Abbey, near Dover, was reputedly the first religious house in the country to be dissolved, when Cromwell's commissioner visited and found the abbot in bed with his mistress. It had an annual revenue of only £56, and a local man bought the tumbledown buildings.

Sometimes the closures really did support the defence of the realm. Faversham Abbey, founded by King Stephen and chosen by him as his last resting place, was demolished and much of the stone taken to France, where it was used to strengthen the fortifications at Calais. Stone from St Radigund's Abbey near Dover was used to build Sandgate Castle.

More usual was the outcome at St Martin's Priory in Dover, where townsmen plundered the buildings for gravestones, altar stones, tiles and timber, leaving just a few structures standing which were used as barns. Combwell Priory near Goudhurst, the convent at Malling, one of the richest in the country, and the nunnery at Sandwich were all sold by the Crown. The final act was the transformation of the great cathedral priories of Canterbury and Rochester into secular cathedral chapters, but not before Becket's shrine had been looted and destroyed. One remarkable survivor was the Carmelite monastery at Aylesford which, although suppressed and sold to the Kent poet Sir Thomas Wyatt, survived through the centuries as a private house until the order was able to buy in back in 1949.

The rejection of the Pope as head of the Church and of Catherine of Aragon as Queen of England had international as well as national repercussions. The Holy Roman Emperor and the King of France sided with the papacy, who believed that England should be brought back to the Roman Catholic fold, by force if necessary. Faced with the threat of invasion,

Sandgate Castle as it was at the beginning of the twentieth century. Undermined by severe storms in 1927 and 1950, over a third of it has been lost to the sea. (Author's collection)

Henry decided to improve his coastal defenses and in just two years, from 1538 to 1540, built a string of castles from Yorkshire to Cornwall. Four of these, at Walmer, Deal, Sandown and Sandgate, were in Kent.

Walmer and Deal castles are pretty much identical, each built in stone-clad brick in the form of a rose, the solitary entrance protected by a portcullis and drawbridge across the outer moat. Walmer Castle gradually metamorphosed into a place of residence, and in the eighteenth century was adapted to provide accommodation for the Lord Warden of the Cinque Ports. The Duke of Wellington, holder of the post in the nineteenth century, died while in residence there. Deal Castle saw no action under the Tudors, but during the Civil War it was held, briefly, by Royalist rebels against Parliament. Sandown Castle, west of Deal, was probably similarly built, but has long since fallen victim to the sea, leaving only a few stones to proclaim its existence.

Further along the coast, between Folkestone and Hythe, Sandgate Castle still stands, though radically modified. Built on a different pattern, roughly a triangle with elliptical sides, it was altered during the Napoleonic Wars to conform to the design of the neighboring Martello towers, but has been badly battered by the sea over the centuries.

Meanwhile, Henry was continuing to accumulate wives. Almost immediately after the execution of Anne Boleyn, he married Jane Seymour, who died giving birth to the long awaited male heir, Edward. Henry took a dislike to his next wife, Anne of Cleves, when he first met her in Rochester and dislike turned to revulsion on their wedding night. The unconsummated marriage was annulled six months later and the man who had arranged it, Thomas Cromwell, was beheaded on Tower Hill on 28 July 1640.

Henry did not attend the execution, as he was busy that day getting married again, this time to Catherine Howard, a cousin of Anne Boleyn. Catherine, not yet 20, was already sexually experienced when she married the king, and she continued to extend her experience after the wedding. Her affair with the handsome courtier Thomas Culpeper of Higham Park near Canterbury seems to have started within the year. They were not discreet, and to compound matters, Catherine employed another former lover as her secretary. By December 1641, the heads of both men were displayed on London Bridge, and Catherine lost her own life early the next year.

Henry died while married to his sixth wife, Catherine Parr, in 1547. The heir, Edward VI, was only 9 years old and his uncle, the Duke of Somerset, acted for him as Lord Protector, assisted by the new king's godfather, Archbishop Cranmer. Now the reformation of the Church really started.

Henry had been quite conservative in religious matters, and his Supremacy did not mean that the Church changed its way of worshipping. In the first year of Edward's reign, almost all the traditional customs and ceremonies were banned: cults of saints, processions, roods, stained glass, vestments and vessels. Wall paintings in churches were obliterated and English bibles and a prayer book brought in. There were mixed reactions in Kent. At Sandhurst, near Hawkhurst, the parishioners welcomed the changes but complained that their minister was not sufficiently zealous. The church's images had been taken down but not defaced, and the processional cross, though no longer used, was stored behind the altar, in full view of the horrified congregation. At Deal, though, the minister flatly refused to believe that somehow the miraculous transformation of bread and wine, in which he had always believed, was no longer happening.

Edward died aged 15, and was succeeded by his half-sister Mary, who was as fervently Roman Catholic as Edward had been Protestant and who

The plaque in Maidstone commemorating seven Protestant martyrs who were burned nearby.
(Anne Thompson)

intended to take her country back to the true faith. All the religious legislation of Edward's reign was immediately repealed, and Cranmer was dismissed as Archbishop of Canterbury and sent to the Tower.

Mary was 38 years old, but despite her age she felt it to be her sacred duty to try to provide an heir to maintain the Catholic succession. Her choice of Prince Philip of Spain as her husband, with its implications of the sovereignty or interference of a foreign power, appalled many even among her supporters. Diffuse rumblings of discontent eventually crystallised in a rebellion in Kent led by Thomas Wyatt, son of the poet.

Establishing his headquarters at his home Allington Castle, Wyatt published a declaration which laid emphasis on the importance of 'liberty and commonwealth' to the English people, which were, he said, being threatened by 'the queen's determinate pleasure to marry with a stranger'.

Then, in January 1554, at the head of about 3,000 men, he marched through Gravesend and Dartford to Blackheath and from there to the gates of London. The capital's inhabitants did not share his views, and 20,000 of them came to the defence of their city and their queen.

Faced with impossible odds, Wyatt's supporters abandoned him and he was executed in March. Mary married Philip in July. Now, with the help of a Catholic husband, Mary could start her God-given task of ridding her realm of the taint of heresy. The burnings started the next year.

In Kent, eighteen women and thirty-six men died for their beliefs, ordinary people like Nicholas Wade, a Dartford linen-weaver; John Newton, a Maidstone pewterer; Edmund Allin, a Frittenden miller; the 'blind maid' known only as Elizabeth; Nicholas Hall, of Dartford, a bricklayer; and the four women burnt together at Canterbury in 1556, 'singing psalms while flames spread about their ears'. Cranmer was burned in Oxford. Their inheritance was, for centuries afterwards, a deep-seated fear and loathing of Catholicism as both dangerous and anti-English. It became a fugitive faith.

Mary died, childless, in 1558, and was succeeded by Anne Boleyn's daughter, Elizabeth, who quickly established a compromise in religious matters, although recusant Catholics were still harassed. Her reign was largely peaceful, and matters of national politics did not intrude often into Kent life until the national emergency created in 1588 by the threat of the Spanish Armada.

Philip II of Spain, formerly the husband of Queen Mary, had not forgotten the Pope's aim of returning England to the Catholic faith, and as his armies now occupied the Netherlands, he saw the perfect opportunity to invade England using a two-pronged approach: his Armada would sail from Spain and defeat resistance in the English Channel and the Duke of Parma's Dutch-based forces could then make the crossing unopposed. In August 1588, the Armada set sail, and watchers on England's coast marked its progress with flares and beacons. A squadron of thirty ships was stationed in the stretch of the English Channel off the Kent coast known as the Downs and men of the local trained bands were put on standby.

One group of 4,000 'soldiers' gathered at Northbourne, although only 500 of them were actually trained and fully armed with muskets and pikes. The rest had a mixture of whatever they could lay hands on – bows, halberds and billhooks, together with a variety of firearms. There were also 700-odd horsemen and about 1,000 pioneers, unarmed labourers who could be used for building earthworks or fetching and carrying. Another 2,000 men were posted between Canterbury and Faversham and nearly 3,000 more just south of Maidstone.

Harassed by English ships, the Armada made its way down the Channel. On 5 August, the Kent commander, Sir Thomas Scott, moved the Northbourne contingent down to the coast to intimidate the enemy, who fortunately could not see the ill-equipped bands close up. Two days later the ships that had been waiting in the Downs joined battle and fireships were sent amongst the Spanish vessels. Providentially, the wind changed direction, and the mighty Armada was driven into the North Sea, pursued by the English. The invasion threat was over.

Be that as it may, Scott was taking no chances, and on hearing that the intention had been to land the Duke of Parma's troops in Dungeness, he hastily redeployed his men there, just in case. A little later, 2,000 of his troops were sent to Tilbury to defend the capital and their sovereign lady, the queen. There, on 19 August 1588, she appeared before them. Supremely aware of the power of spectacle, she wore a plumed helmet and a steel cuirass over a white velvet gown and rode a pure white horse (or possibly a dappled grey one: accounts vary), telling them 'I know I have the body of a weak and feeble woman, but I have the heart and stomach of a king'. Her status as Gloriana, a national icon, was now unassailable.

Elizabeth died in 1603 and was succeeded with no great opposition by the only person who had any real claim to the throne, James VI of Scotland, who became James I of England, the first Stuart monarch.

James was a conundrum: he loved the hunt, and theological disputation, and drink, and sermonising, and women, and masques, and beautiful young men. One of the latter, the very beautiful George Villiers, Duke of Buckingham, was James's last favourite, but his good looks were not matched by any vestige of talent for the great offices which James heaped upon him. As a diplomat, his arrogance scuttled James's hopes of marrying the Spanish infanta to his son Charles; as a soldier his disastrous military campaigns in France and Spain were ruinous in terms of money and lives lost. None of this stopped James's successor, Charles I, from maintaining

Buckingham in positions of power and he was allowed to buy from Edward Zouche, for £1,000, the office of Lord Warden of the Cinque Ports. The post was granted for life, but Zouche needed the money to finance the splendid mansion he was renovating in Hampshire.

By tradition, although not by right, the Lord Warden nominated the Members of Parliament for the Cinque Ports, who dutifully elected them as their representatives. This gave him a fair amount of political clout, since his nominees would do as they were told in the Commons. In 1625, for Charles I's first Parliament, Buckingham had a moderate success, with three members of his household getting seats, but the Ports stopped cooperating and he could not repeat the feat in 1626. Never popular, his reputation in the country had reached rock-bottom, and there was also a mysterious delay in getting his written nominations out to the Ports. Five men to whom the duke had promised seats were disappointed. It was a disaster, and worse was to follow. Shortly after Parliament opened, one of his nominees decided to sit for another constituency, and another was elevated to the peerage. This left Buckingham with only one man in the Commons.

He did little better in the 1628 election, and finally bowed to criticism of his tenure of so many high offices and resigned as Lord Warden. This was too little too late, and his assassination by a disgruntled army officer later that year was the occasion of national rejoicing.

Charles I appointed another of his father's lovely young men to the Lieutenancy of Kent. The Earl of Pembroke's 'comeliness' had first attracted James to him, but his only gifts were to understand horses and dogs. Fortunately, as he was also foul-mouthed and bad-tempered, he rarely visited Kent and left most of the governing of the county to his deputies. His eventual break with Charles in 1641, however, came about not because of his political ineptitude, but over religion.

Pembroke was a Puritan, one of a group of people within the Church who believed that it needed reforming, with less ritual, more preaching and a greater focus on the bible. The king, and the man he appointed Archbishop of Canterbury, William Laud, wanted more ritual, less preaching and a return to 'the beauty of holiness' in church services. Many Puritans thought the Laudians were closet Catholics and that the king was in thrall to his Catholic queen.

They also tended to support attempts to limit what they saw as the king's abuse of power during the 1630s, and when, in 1640, after a twelve-year period of personal rule, Charles called two parliaments in quick succession, they formed a clear majority of the MPs. Kent was no exception. The Cinque Ports were subject to huge pressure from the new Lord Warden, the king's cousin the Duke of Lennox, but withstood his bullying tactics to return a majority of men who now called themselves Parliamentarians.

Charles wanted this Parliament to vote him money, but it had other priorities: their own privileges and the king's abuses of power and religion. One of its first acts was to impeach the reforming Archbishop of Canterbury for high treason. His reforms and brutal methods of enforcing them – branding or ear clipping, for example – had made him a hate figure to Puritans everywhere. Parliament's demands began to impact seriously on the king's ability

The Christ Gate at Canterbury Cathedral where the Puritan Richard Culmer pulled down the large stone image of Christ. It took several men some hours. (Anne Thompson)

to govern as he wished and when he ill-advisedly arrived at the House of Commons in person to arrest five of its members for treason, in gross violation of parliamentary privilege, breaking point was reached. Charles left London on 10 January 1642 and set up his court in Oxford, where he began raising an army, having declared that Parliament was in rebellion. The Civil War had started.

Kent was under parliamentary control throughout the Civil War. None of the major battles was fought in the county and it was spared most of the horrors of Englishmen slaughtering each other and the inevitable looting and retaliation that followed each confrontation.

Being under parliamentary control did not mean that there was blanket support for Parliament, which was strongest in urban centres. Ashford, Canterbury and Cranbrook had raised volunteer forces for Parliament even before the war began. In Canterbury, the radical Puritan Richard Culmer supervised the destruction of the cathedral's 'idolatrous' stained glass, and pulled down statues and images. Parliament's soldiers broke up the altar rails for firewood.

In the countryside, Royalist support was greater. Sir John Sackville of Knole House was arrested and taken to London along with five wagon loads of arms, which, it was said, were intended for Royalist use. Arms were seized at Cobham Hall and Hothfield and the houses of lesser gentry were ransacked. In 1643, emboldened by a surge in Royalist fortunes, anti-parliamentarian rebels, mostly yeomen and craftsmen, began to gather at Ightham, Sevenoaks, Aylesford and Faversham. Hopelessly outnumbered, they were defeated at Tonbridge in July. The next year, 500 Kent men, conscripted to Parliament's New Model Army rebelled at Wrotham, and even in parliamentarian Canterbury there were riots in 1647 when the mayor tried to enforce Parliament's ban on celebrating Christmas.

In 1648, with the king under arrest on the Isle of Wight, the Royalists staged one last desperate campaign. The Downs fleet mutinied and was rumoured to be sailing to the Isle of Wight to rescue Charles and bring him to Kent, where Royalists rallied to the cause. Sir Richard Hardres seized Deal and Walmer castles and by May claimed to have 11,000 men at his disposal. Parliament responded by sending in General Fairfax and the battle-hardened men of the New Model Army. They defeated Sir William

The spot where Charles II made his triumphant return to English soil is commemorated on Dover seafront. He had to listen to several lengthy loyal speeches before he was allowed to leave. (Anne Thompson)

Brockman of Beachborough Hall at the Battle of Maidstone and routed Sir Richard Hardres at Canterbury. It was the end of the Royalist cause. Charles I was executed on 30 January 1649.

Throughout the interregnum and Protectorate of Oliver Cromwell, Kent was seen as a potential threat to the government because of its proximity to Europe, where most of the Royalists exiles had fled. Suspected Royalist sympathisers were routinely rounded up and interrogated, but their fortitude was rewarded when the experiment with republicanism collapsed with Cromwell's death, and Charles II made a triumphant return to English soil at Dover.

After kneeling to kiss his home soil on Dover beach, Charles's journey to London through Kent took four days, while the people all very wisely sent messages of congratulation, made loyal addresses and gave gifts. These were soon followed by scores of petitions from Royalists reminding Charles of their sacrifices and asking for compensation. There was some retribution against parliamentarians, too. Sir Henry Vane of Shipbourne was exceuted in 1662, and the former governor of Dover Castle, Algernon Sidney, fled abroad to continue plotting against the king until his own execution in 1683.

One of the new king's first acts was to appoint his brother James, Duke of York as Lord High Admiral and Lord Warden of the Cinque Ports. In 1665, Charles declared war on the Dutch, who had risen over the seventeenth century to the status of economic superpower, and were threatening English trade and prosperity. Under the Duke of York the war did not go well for the navy, and culminated in a humiliating defeat in 1667 when the

Dutch fleet bombarded and then captured the town of Sheerness, then sailed up the Medway to Chatham, where they burned thirteen ships and towed away the *Royal Charles*, the English flagship. It was one of the worst defeats in the Royal Navy's history.

This same Duke of York succeeded to the throne as James II in 1685. His brother Charles had been received into the Catholic Church on his deathbed, but James had long been candid in confessing his Catholicism. His heirs were his Protestant daughters by his first wife, but when a Catholic son was born to his second wife in 1688, the English fear of a Catholic succession overcame their support of the restored monarchy. A group of nobles invited James's daughter Mary and her husband William of Orange to take the throne.

When William landed in the West Country, James decided to flee, but on the Kent coast was arrested by a gang of fishermen and imprisoned in Faversham for several days. Finally the last Stuart monarch was allowed to take ship at Rochester and to live out his life in exile.

A plaque marks the house where James II was held for three days, in a Faversham brewery and public house. It must have been a novel experience for him. (Anne Thompson)

Five

ORDINARY LIVES

The great affairs of kings and queens did not often encroach on the lives of the ordinary people of Kent. Like people anywhere at any time, they were mostly concerned with the mundane matters of staying alive, getting a living and somewhere to live, and raising their children.

Kent was a largely rural county, the ninth largest in England, covering just 400,000 hectares. Until about 1500, only Canterbury was an urban centre of any significance, but in the sixteenth century, trade links with the continent and proximity to the burgeoning capital, London, led to rapid urban growth, especially around the estuaries of the Medway and Thames. By 1700, perhaps a third of Kent's people lived in towns, although these were generally tiny by modern standards, with fewer than 2,000 inhabitants. New towns were emerging, too. Deal grew as a result of the naval yard established there and Tunbridge Wells developed around the fashionable spa.

Townspeople provided goods and services to their country cousins. Rural folk could export their goods through the ports or collect their coal which had been sent down from Newcastle. They could go to the market, or visit the shops and makers of clothing, metal and leather goods and food. They could do business, visit the inns, see performances by travelling players (including perhaps Shakespeare himself: he is known to have travelled to Kent with the Lord Chamberlain's Men in 1605), or play the fashionable game of bowls. Canterbury and Tonbridge catered for the leisured classes with goldsmiths, booksellers and clock- and watch-makers.

In the countryside, innumerable villages and hamlets were scattered across a largely pastoral landscape of enclosed fields. The Weald, once

Romney Marsh sheep are now recognised as a distinct breed, with desirable long wool and meat renowned for its flavour. (Anne Thompson)

heavily wooded, had been extensively cleared to provide charcoal for industry. The marshes had been drained. Wealden men grazed their sheep on the Romney Marsh in summer, hiring local men as 'lookers' to tend their flocks. The population here was depleted, badly affected by plague and malaria. It was known to be a very 'aguish' place, but the countless little waterways which criss-crossed the land and attracted the mosquitoes also provided a stock of fish and wildfowl for food.

Kent's reputation as the Garden of England started with the Tudors, although some fruit, especially cherries, had been grown in monastic gardens in the county. Presumably Henry VIII, having destroyed the monasteries and their gardens, noticed the lack of cherries on the royal dessert plate, as he gave his fruiterer, Richard Harris, 42 hectares of land near Teynham on which to create the country's first large fruit collection. By the end of the century it had become 'the chief mother of all other orchards' in England. Royal example stimulated consumption in fashionable circles, which in turn led to new orchards. Within fifty years, Kent's orchards were renowned throughout Europe. An increasing number of fruiterers created their own; others travelled to Kent before harvest to purchase the prospective crops of cherries, pears, medlars, pippins and other apples while they were still on the tree.

The sixteenth century also saw the growth of the other archetypal Kent crop, hops. Used for flavouring beer, which kept better than ale, hops were suited to the soil around Sittingbourne, Canterbury and Maidstone. By 1655, a third of all the hops produced in England were from the county and local brewers profited. Britain's oldest brewery, Shepherd Neame, was founded in Faversham in 1698. The other essential ingredient of beer, malt, was widely produced and used by local brewers or exported through the ports. Nearly half of London's imports of malt in the seventeenth century came from Kent through Sandwich, Dover and Faversham.

The woollen industry in the Weald around Cranbrook began to be overtaken by the 'new draperies' produced in East Kent by immigrants from the Low Countries. They made cheaper, more colourful cloth than Cranbrook Grey, at first in Sandwich and later in Canterbury. The Canterbury drapers began to diversify into ribbons and lace, and the arrival of French Huguenot refugees in the 1680s with their silk-weaving skills boosted the industry. In

The 'French Church' in the crypt of Canterbury Cathedral. A service in French is still held there every Sunday. (Author's collection)

The Church House at Throwley, near Faversham, a typical Wealden hall house with a hipped roof. (Author's collection)

Maidstone, the linked trade of thread-twisting provided employment for hundreds of men and women.

These French-speaking immigrants wanted to worship in their own language, and in Sandwich were given their own church, St Peter's. They were so numerous in Canterbury that they were allocated the west end of the crypt of Canterbury Cathedral for their services.

If a man had work, whether on the land or in the town, and could support his family, life could be tolerably good, though not without a host of perils which could destroy a household in a day. Wages in Kent were higher than elsewhere in the country and with London and the fishing ports competing for available labour, an able-bodied man could take his pick.

Having secured employment, he next needed shelter. The homes of the poorest day-labourers were little more than shacks; even those a little better-off, with permanent employment, lived in single or two-roomed houses which were not expected to last for more than a generation. A tradesman or yeoman could afford something better, a house with a parlour and perhaps separate rooms upstairs. In Kent these traditional dwellings, Wealden hall houses, survive in surprisingly large numbers.

They were timber framed, usually in oak, with walls infilled with wattle and daub. Glass had become cheap enough to be used widely by the end of the sixteenth century when glazed windows replaced internal sliding shutters. Brick, at first only used for chimney stacks, was the most common material for new builds by the end of the seventeenth century.

The medieval houses were simple halls with a central hearth open to the thatched roof, through which the smoke escaped. Later, the hall was divided up to include a parlour which was primarily a sleeping room. Often the blocks at either end of the house had a first-floor room or rooms over them, with access by means of a ladder or staircase.

During the sixteenth century, householders started to add chimney stacks and ceilings in the halls, creating a whole upper storey which could be heated by individual fires. Dormer windows were put in to maximise the light. The style was adopted for new houses in the seventeenth century.

Thatch was very widely used. It was economical and readily available; extras such as drainpipes and guttering were unnecessary and cheap walls and rafters could easily support the light thatching material. Its major drawback was the risk of fire.

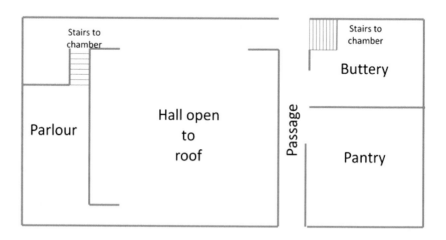

The floor plan of a typical early Wealden hall house with a central fireplace. (Author's collection)

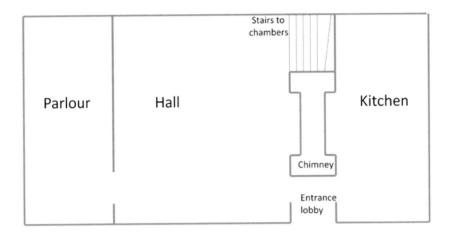

How a Wealden hall house was often altered from the sixteenth century to provide two storeys and more fireplaces. (Author's collection)

Most Kent towns by the sixteenth century had public water supplies created by diverting streams or springs to public conduits or wells, and town authorities generally provided leather fire buckets for fire-fighting. In 1681, the town of Faversham even bought a fire engine with a pump. These measures were unfortunately quite inadequate once a fire had taken hold. In 1661, Sandwich gaol and court house burnt down; in 1672, fire destroyed Westbere vicarage, barn, stables, church steeple and most of the church; and eleven shops were burnt down in a single night in Tunbridge Wells causing damage worth over £2,500. In London, at least, it began to be possible to insure against fire by the end of the seventeenth century, but the practice was slow to reach the provinces. Affected people could, however, apply to the county justices if they were left destitute. In 1653, Thomas Wetton, a Cranbrook labourer who had provided for his old age by buying three houses and seen them all destroyed, was given compensation, as were John Driver, father and son of Chevening, whose adjoining houses were burnt down, leaving their wives and children destitute.

Men and women of the medieval and early modern periods were much more likely to marry than not, usually in their mid to late twenties. Marriage was necessary for economic survival for a woman and for a modicum of domestic comfort for a man. It almost inevitably brought children, although many of these would not see their first birthday. If they did survive the myriad dangers of early childhood, their education became of concern to their parents.

The poorest children could not expect any schooling at all; a degree of prosperity was required to release a child from the necessity of working to put bread on the table as soon as he or she could. A yeoman or tradesman was often able to give his sons, and occasionally his daughters, some sort of formal education. The opportunities for future employment were greatly enhanced by having at least basic numeracy and literacy.

Schoolmasters in Kent were licensed by the Diocese of Canterbury and were very often in holy orders in their parish. Teaching commonly took place in the church itself, as in the chapel of Eastbridge Hospital, Canterbury. Reading was taught first, and then, at about the age of 7 or 8, writing. By that age, children were becoming useful in the workplace, and many would not have learnt to write beyond a signature or just an initial.

For the better-off there were grammar schools after elementary education, and there was a good selection in Kent. Cranbrook, Maidstone, Dartford, Faversham, Ashford, Rochester, Sevenoaks and Sandwich all had grammar schools, usually endowed by benevolent patrons, although Maidstone's school was founded by virtue of its charter. The education provided was for boys only, and focused on Latin and Greek, necessities for the legal profession or the Church. The cost of sending a boy to the King's School in Canterbury was about £12 a year in the seventeenth century, probably typical, but to this had to be added the loss of a boy's contribution to the family income. It was beyond the reach of most.

If a man was without employment, the prospects for his family could be grim. Until the Dissolution, monasteries were the providers of succour to the poor, and to travellers, lepers or pilgrims. Hospitals to provide for their needs were also set up by individual churches, to fulfil their Christian duty, or by the rich, seeking to ease their path to heaven. Some included an oratory where prayers for the deceased founder would, it was intended, be sung in perpetuity. The Poor Priests' Hospital in Canterbury combined both these ends in one building, by providing lodgings for destitute clerics who in return prayed daily for the souls of their benefactors. The idea of the almshouse, often called the Maison Dieu, was developed from hospitals to

The original home of Norton Knatchbull School, Ashford, founded by Sir Norton Knatchbull in 1630 with an endowment of £30 per annum. It still exists, in other premises, as a boys' grammar school. (Anne Thompson)

provide long-term care for the disabled and aged infirm. As leprosy began to recede in the fourteenth century, some leper houses became almshouses.

Archbishop Lanfranc's Hospital of St John the Baptist in Canterbury was followed by several more in the city. Although the inmates of the hospitals were saved from poverty and homelessness, the price they paid was the loss of freedom. They had to wear a uniform, were not allowed to leave the premises without permission, and were punished for such misdemeanors as being quarrelsome. Children were rarely admitted. Pilfering seems always to have been a problem, with inmates selling off the hospitals' property outside. One hospital in Canterbury was forced to fit a triple lock to its money chest, with three keys held by three different people.

Leper hospitals always had a funding problem, as no one liked to be too closely associated with them. In Rochester, Gundulf's hospital for lepers was supported by grants and revenues of lands settled upon it, but still needed extra donations from the cathedral purse and kitchens. When a new archbishop was installed, the lepers also had the right to collect alms from those present at his table and when the banquet was over got the table-cloth too. As was the case in many lazar houses, the prior was sometimes a leper himself.

Because many of the hospitals and almshouses in Kent were in lay or Church hands, rather than run by religious orders, a lot survived the Dissolution. St Bartholomew's in Rochester continued as an independent charity, but with only a small income from the estates settled on it, it slid into poverty, until the development of a royal dockyard at Chatham brought prosperity to the area. The meagre estates then became so valuable that the Crown unsuccessfully tried twice to seize them. St John's Hospital at Hythe was conveyed by the Church to the corporation to be run by the jurats as an almshouse. Others were lost. St Bartholomew's lazar house at Dover was

Founded by Henry III in 1234, the monks of the Maison Dieu at Ospringe were required to offer hospitality to poor and needy travellers and pilgrims and to keep a room ready for the king's use. (Anne Thompson)

torn down and St Mary's, the Maison Dieu, became a victualling yard; Corpus Christi fraternity almshouse in Maidstone was used as a school. The hospital of St Mary at Ospringe was an early victim of Henry VIII's revenue raising exercises. In 1519, he ordered it to be dissolved and its revenues and possessions used to endow St John's College, Cambridge. The building became a public house.

The hospitals and almshouses had fulfilled the biblical exhortation to feed the hungry and welcome the stranger. They may not always have performed this duty wholeheartedly, but they usually provided a safety net for the very poorest. Now, in some parts of the county, there was nothing at all to stop their fall into destitution and starvation.

There were a lot of poor people by Elizabeth's reign, for the simple reason that the population was increasing. Many of the deprived and unemployed took to the roads, looking for food and work. In 1593, William Lambarde complained of Kent that the county was 'overspread not only with unpunished swarms of idle rogues and of counterfeit soldiers but also with numbers of poor and weak but unpitied servitors'. At Preston, a small village near Faversham, the parish records show in 1596 the christening of 'Thomasin Johns, the daughter of a poor woman delivered in the vicar's stable'; in the same year the burial of 'a poor woman, wife of John Wilkinson. She died in the vicar's barn'; and in 1598 the baptism of 'Barbara daughter of John Cooper of Evare who was born under a hedge'.

Most vagrants, however, were young men, in search of work, but generally finding only hostility. They were suspected of thieving and murdering as well as being filthy and sinful. The government responded to their desperation by introducing a law in 1572 to allow for a vagrant to be punished by being whipped and 'being burned through the gristle of the right ear with a hot iron'. If this didn't cure him of his vagrancy, he could be hanged. People were to be punished for taking vagrants into their houses, which might encourage others to take to the road. In 1598, William Higgenson of Brook, a labourer, was fined for taking in Joan Jynner and giving her work.

Part of the problem was that most towns and villages had enough of their own poor to deal with, without taking on any strangers. The law finally got round to addressing this in 1597, with 'An Act for the Relief of the Poor'. Parishes, funded by a tax on parishioners, had to look after destitute children;

workhouses and hospitals should be provided to accommodate the poor; vagrants, and anyone not born in the parish, were to be whipped and sent back from whence they came. This was not always successful. In 1654, Philip North was whipped as a vagrant at Gillingham and sent to his alleged birthplace Faversham, where he was whipped and sent back to Gillingham, where he was whipped again before being sent to – Faversham. In 1691, a woman was found wandering in the Ashford area speaking only 'a sort of Scottish language'. Since no one could understand her, she could not be sent anywhere.

To modern sensibilities the law was particularly harsh on children, who, for the purposes of the vagrancy laws, were treated as adults. In 1613, Katherine Rolfe, an orphan child, was ricocheted between Hythe and Dover while the authorities argued about which of them had responsibility for her. Nearly sixty years later John Lacy, whose parents had scraped a living selling brooms in Saltwood, was orphaned. The locals decided that John was not their responsibility, but that of New Romney. He was duly whipped and sent there. The overseers of New Romney refused to accept him and sent him back, although after a year of haggling, they finally conceded defeat. John Lacy was 6 years old.

Some towns did build hospitals and almshouses to replace those lost at the Dissolution. Smith's Hospital in Canterbury was founded by John and Anne Smith in 1644 to give thanks for the gift of a son, born after twenty years and four months of childless marriage. Mary Honywood endowed the almshouses in Lenham in 1633, and Thomas Philipott did the same in Eltham in 1682. Other towns were able to use the old religious buildings, as happened in Sandwich and Hythe.

Poverty led inevitably to criminality, and many convicted criminals were recorded as of no fixed abode or place of work. Their crimes were mostly related to thefts, usually of money, clothes or animals. In 1595, for example, a soldier and two London men seeking harvest work broke into a house at Sutton-at-Hone and stole a woman's gown and petticoat, and sheets, aprons and handkerchiefs, presumably to sell. One of them had left London with only sixpence in his pocket, and was flat broke by the time he reached Sutton. At the same time, three soldiers returning from France with only seven shillings between them stole a bible and service book from Charing church. (They said that they had been hoping to lift the church plate.)

Men and women in low-paid work were convicted of theft if driven to it or the temptation was strong enough. Mostly these were petty thefts, but in 1600 two Bobbing labourers dug up thirty-five cherry trees from a neighbour's orchard. They must have had a quick sale in mind, evidence of the value of the Kent fruit trade.

Criminals, once arrested, could expect to be confined for a time in town gaols, which were little more than insanitary lock-ups. Once convicted, punishments were cheap and quick to carry out. Death was the penalty for all felonies, although first offenders were sometimes branded. Petty larceny was punished by whipping and lesser misdemeanours by the pillory, ducking stool and stocks.

Although there was a gallows at Canterbury Castle, the main Kent site for executions was at Penenden Heath near Maidstone. It was a conveniently large site, as hangings drew large and often unruly crowds. Whipping was carried out either behind a moving cart for a specified distance, or at a whipping post. In 1634, Joan Banks was sentenced in Maidstone to be tied to 'a cart's tail' and whipped from the gaol to the bridge. In Chatham, in 1681, Richard Weston and John Price, who had stolen brass from the dockyard, were sentenced to be publicly whipped 'until their bodies do bleed'.

The stocks, pillory and ducking stool involved making a public example of the wrongdoer. The pillory was less often used than the stocks, but anyone caught bewitching cattle had to stand in it, whereas the ducking stool was mostly used for scolds and troublemakers. Its use was probably not widespread, since it required the nearby presence of a suitably deep body of water. However, there was certainly one at Deptford, on the confluence of the Thames and the Ravensbourne, in 1688, for 'the correcting and well-governing of idle, lewd and disorderly women and others', and another at Fordwich on the River Stour, fitted to a crane on the wharf by the Court Hall.

Some crimes for which punishments were meted out are thankfully no longer on the statute books: travelling on the Sabbath, say, or adultery as a capital offence. Witchcraft is another example, although prosecutions in the county were less common than elsewhere. In 1645, four Faversham women were convicted of witchcraft. Their leader said she had made a pact with the Devil, signed in her own blood, and in return the Evil One regularly left small sums of money in her house during the night. This claim was something of a novelty in English witch trials and attracted much attention. The women were all found guilty and hanged.

In 1652, twelve men and six women from Cranbrook and the Isle of Grain stood trial in Maidstone accused of witchcraft. It was alleged that they had ruined fields of wheat, bewitched sheep and brought about the deaths of horses, pigs and children. Two of the women admitted freely that they had slept with the Devil and three said that they were pregnant by him. The pregnancies were as imaginary as the satanic sex, but six of the accused, all women, were found guilty and hanged.

Fewer than twenty women of Kent were executed for witchcraft during the sixteenth and seventeenth centuries, a fraction of the number condemned by the 'Witchfinder General', Matthew Hopkins. Fortunately for elderly poor women in Kent, he never visited the county.

The pest house at Great Chart. Built in the fifteenth century, it was used after the First World War as a museum. (Anne Thompson)

Sickness could not always be blamed on witches. The outbreaks of bubonic plague which regularly swept across the country were often attributed to divine displeasure for the sins of mankind. These were many and various and included swearing, negligence in attending church, play-going, covetousness, and extravagant female fashion. Alternatively, comets were to blame (there were three in 1618 alone), or eclipses of the sun.

Plague could not be cured so had to be managed. In 1578, the government issued Plague Orders, which with some modifications were in effect until 1666. Local magistrates were to raise a tax for the relief of the sick, order the burning of the clothes and bedding of victims, and funerals were to take place at dusk to deter onlookers – corpses were still highly contagious. Houses where there was suspected infection were to be shut up for six weeks with all the members of the family, sick or healthy, locked inside, or the sick were to be removed to a quarantined pest house.

Cranbrook had a pest house, still standing, as did Kemsing. Canterbury used Bowling Green Alley near St Mildred's church, and a building next to Great Chart church is traditionally held to have been the village pest house. Sandwich appointed a pest master to take care of their house and tend to the sick.

Other towns simply incarcerated the sick in their homes. In 1625, in Ashford, the family of Richard Cole were quarantined, and shut up with them was John Longley, a bachelor. One summer evening, still in good health, he evaded the town's watchmen and made his way to a field at Ham Street, to be met, at a distance, by two relatives and a friend. From his field, John shouted his last will and testament to his brother-in-law, Nicholas Mount, who wrote down for him how he wanted his debts paid and to whom he left his property. Then John honourably went back to Ashford and, in August, to death.

Towns suffered particularly from bubonic plague. Kent's ports were especially vulnerable: 10 per cent of Dover's population was lost in the outbreak of 1625–26, and Chatham probably lost a third of its inhabitants in the last outbreak of 1665–66. Migration into towns from the countryside filled the gaps, with incomers soon making up more than half the population of most towns. There was considerable geographical mobility in the sixteenth and seventeenth centuries, and plague spread quickly across the country, spread by legitimate travellers as well as tramping men.

There were three major thoroughfares in Kent, all starting in the capital. One ran from London to Dover on Watling Street via Canterbury; another to Hythe via New Cross, Maidstone and Ashford, and the third to Rye through Bromley and Tonbridge. Seventeenth-century maps show side roads, too, which suggests that these were passable, in dry weather at least.

Roads were not metalled and only occasionally paved and their repair was the responsibility of each parish. Their response to this duty was mixed, and the Kent quarter sessions records of the seventeenth century are littered with complaints of overgrown hedges, mud or muck outside farms, decayed wooden bridges, landslip and overhanging trees. Where the road passed through private land, its repair fell to the landowner who might, or might not, take his obligations seriously. If the road divided two fields, the farmer sometimes ploughed straight across it, 'forgetting' that it was there; sometimes he took action to block the road, by demolishing a bridge for example, and in one extraordinary case in 1600 Solomon Ware of Horsmonden inexplicably dug a sawpit in the middle of the road to Cranbrook and started to work it.

Animals, as well as goods, were moved along Kent's roads. Sheep and cattle were driven to Smithfield from Romney Marsh or the Weald, and churned up the roads, but surfaces were particularly badly scarred by wagons used for transporting heavy goods. A royal proclamation of 1621 forbade the use of four-wheeled wagons altogether, but it was ignored. In 1662, it was decreed that wheels should be at least 4in wide to stop them rutting the road, and another law forbade more than five horses being used. The laws were mostly flouted, and only the worst offenders prosecuted. In 1630, Stephen and John Smyth, two Dover waggoners, were accused of damaging the King's highway in Chatham, Strood, Frindsbury, Higham, Shorne and Northfleet by carrying loads weighing more than 2 tons and using more than five horses. Such an extensive area of damage suggests that they were persistent offenders. These attempts to fit the traffic to the roads inevitably failed, and improvements did not begin until the problem was addressed the other way round.

People such as chapmen, the travelling salesmen of their day, moving relatively small amounts of goods, used pack horses. They were better than wagons in bad weather, were faster and ate less than wagon horses.

Bridges were built specifically to accommodate them, narrow, but with low parapets so that the horses' panniers were not impeded. In 1615, Hythe Corporation ordered the West Bridge to be made 6ft wide with stone and timber, specifically for pack horses to use. Although this is long gone, there is a surviving example at Eynsford.

For people travelling without goods, the choices were limited. If you were poor, you walked; if you could afford it, you rode. If you did not keep a mount, they could be hired from stables in most towns. Women usually rode pillion. By the 1630s, however, public coaches were working from London to several provincial towns. A network grew up during the 1650s, and passengers could expect to cover 30 to 40 miles a day. Regular coach services left from London inns at advertised times and stopped at others on the way. Those who could pay more sat inside, those who could not, on top. Inns became the passenger and goods stations of their day, where passengers could be met, goods collected and both transferred to feeder services. Kent had ten services a week in 1637, and twenty-two a week in 1681; there was a weekly service from Dover to the White Hart in Southwark, leaving on Thursdays, and a weekly boat service as well.

Waterborne transport was cheaper than land traffic, and as well as the main ports, there were twenty or so little harbours or creeks around the coast which could cope with small vessels. The Medway, Stour and Rother rivers were also partly navigable, so that only a small part of the county was more than 15 miles from a port. Little boats, of less than 90 tonnes, carried to London goods the roads could not cope with: heavy merchandise such as grain, coal, bricks, sand, timber or iron wares. They returned with holds full of the sorts of luxury items only to be obtained in the capital. Margate, Faversham and Rochester exported a great deal of corn, while Faversham sent most of the county's wool to London. Timber, cut in north Kent, left in barges through Erith and Woolwich.

Post was being delivered from London to Dover in the sixteenth century, and in 1635 a royal proclamation empowered Thomas Witherings to set up a new Letter Office, with authority to carry letters for the general public for up to 80 miles for tuppence. During the interregnum, express postal services for official letters were established, with the promise that they would travel at 7mph in summer and 5mph in winter. The next year, the London

Register, Thomas Dunn, expected to receive letters from his deputies in the Kent ports in not much more than twenty-four hours.

In 1660, an Act of Parliament established a General Post Office. Over the next decade by-posts were established to towns off the six post roads, including the London-to-Dover road. The spread of news and gossip could now be very quick indeed.

Travel outside England from Kent meant crossing the Channel from Dover or another of the Cinque Ports still able to act as an anchorage. The journey took three to five hours if the weather was calm, but all sea travel was uncertain. Sea charts were not accurate and the presence of wrecks created another hazard. Lighthouses were few and far between. After the Roman lighthouse in Dover fell into disuse, what little was done to guide sailors was done by the Church. The shrine of Our Lady at Bradstowe (now Broadstairs) kept a light burning in a blue glass lantern for seafarers, and could be seen many miles off shore, and for a while a hermit living in a cave in a cliff near Dover set up a light to guide ships.

At the end of the seventeenth century, an octagonal structure was built on the site of the original North Foreland Lighthouse. (Author's collection)

A major hazard to shipping was the Goodwin Sands, a 16km-long sand-bank in the English Channel about 10km off the town of Deal. To address this, the first purpose-built lighthouse in England since Roman times was erected at the North Foreland, in the east of the Isle of Thanet, in 1499. It consisted of a 6m-high wooden post with a pivot on top. This formed the fulcrum of a long pole with an iron basket full of wood and pitch at one end, and the other end a weighted counterbalance. The basket could be lowered to be refilled and raised again. Variations on this system were tried until 1691, when a stone-built tower, 12m high, was built. A lighthouse at the South Foreland, between Langdon Bay and St Margaret's, followed, and at Dungeness, where the vast flat area of shingle, invisible at night, caused many wrecks.

Six

FIGHTING THE FRENCH

I n April 1689, William and Mary were crowned as joint sovereigns, but James had no intention of going quietly. By 1692, he had secured the assistance of Louis XIV of France and together they gathered a fleet and an army ready to take back James's throne. Although Kent was vulnerable, and the local militias were put on standby, the ships were destroyed by the English fleet a week later, off La Hogue. It was the start of more than a century of hostilities.

For much of the next 120 years Britain was at war with France. The War of the Spanish Succession (1701–14) was succeeded by the War of the Austrian Succession (1740–48), the Seven Years War (1756–63) and the American War of Independence (1775–83) in which the French sided with the colonists. Kent had a respite from invasion threats, however: until Napoleon threatened to attack British soil at the end of the eighteenth century, the battles were fought overseas, and had little local impact.

In fact, the effects of war on the county were generally advantageous. Warfare was now reliant on gunpowder, and governments sought ever more effective machinery to increase its killing power. The use of artillery and handguns at sea as well as on land provided welcome manufacturing opportunities for Kent just as its traditional industries were starting to wane.

The woollen cloth industry round Cranbrook was all but finished. The Canterbury weavers were migrating to Spitalfields, where Huguenot master weavers were now living in smart houses and enjoying the profits made from high-quality velvets, brocades, satins and watered silk. The Maidstone thread twisters, whose market had disappeared, turned instead to twisting imported hemp to be used in hop bagging.

The Woolwich Royal Arsenal at the beginning of the twentieth century. At its peak, during the First World War, it extended over 530 hectares and employed around 80,000 people. (Author's collection)

In their place, new industries designed to feed the war machine sprang up. Woolwich particularly profited. It was a quiet village until the sixteenth century, when Henry VIII founded a dockyard there in 1512. In the early 1700s, Woolwich Dockyard launched more ships that any other English yard.

Woolwich Royal Arsenal was established in 1671, originally as an ordinance storage depot. Then in 1695, an ammunition workshop was built to manufacture gunpowder, shell cases, fuses and paper gun cartridges. The process was undertaken by hand, overseen by a Chief Firemaster. Gun carriages were made nearby.

Next, the Woolwich Brass Foundry was built between 1716 and 1717 when the government had run low on stocks of artillery. The private contractor it used had blown up his own works, himself and his visitors while demonstrating the casting process to several dignitaries. Andrew Schalch, a German master-founder, was appointed to manage the new works. He never allowed the furnaces to be opened until everyone present had joined him in prayer, and craftsmanship and godliness combined to produce brass artillery renowned throughout Europe. The Woolwich Foundry fulfilled most of the army's needs during the American War of Independence.

At the same time, in 1716, two companies of artillery were formed under the auspices of the Board of Ordnance rather than the army, and based at Woolwich. Named the Royal Regiment of Artillery, they provided a versatile workforce at the works, as well as ensuring their security: they were housed in barracks within the compound. In 1720, the Board established an on-site academy for the education of its artillery officers, alongside those of its newly formed Corps of Engineers. An offshoot of the academy was the Royal Military Repository, a collection of 'Military Machines'. Established in 1770, the building housed an educational display of cannons and mortars, and there was a training ground outside to teach skills in handling heavy artillery on various terrains and in different conflict scenarios.

At Chatham, the royal dockyard established by Elizabeth I found itself in decline at the beginning of the eighteenth century, mostly because the Medway was silting up, making navigation difficult. Its regeneration came from its transformation from a refitting base into a building yard. There on 7 May 1765 HMS *Victory* was floated out of the Old Single Dock. After a long and honourable career she achieved lasting fame aged 40 in 1805, as the flagship of Vice-Admiral Nelson in Britain's greatest naval victory, the defeat of the French and Spanish at the Battle of Trafalgar.

In 1922. HMS *Victory* was saved for the nation and placed permanently into dry dock in Portsmouth, where she remains today, the oldest commissioned warship in the world. (Author's collection)

By 1770, the Chatham Dockyard was vast, stretching 1.5km in length and covering an area in excess of 384,000 sq. m. At the turn of the eighteenth century it was employing over 1,600 men, including shipwrights, blockmakers, caulkers, pitch-heaters, blacksmiths, joiners, carpenters, sail makers, riggers and ropemakers.

Faversham and Dartford, meanwhile, capitalised on the demand for gunpowder. Several small works in Faversham had amalgamated into a single plant, the 'Home Works', which was taken over by the government in 1759. It became the Chart Gunpowder Mill, the oldest of its kind in the world, and supplied gunpowder for the battles of Waterloo and Trafalgar. A second factory a little west of the town became a leading supplier to the British East India Company, by this time starting out on its subjugation of the subcontinent. In Dartford, a paper mill was converted for the production of gunpowder, and other entrepreneurs joined the bandwagon. By 1790, there were four mills and twenty years later the powder magazines at Dartford were the most extensive in England.

Gunpowder was made from saltpetre, charcoal and sulphur. On site, the ingredients were processed individually and then combined in isolated mixing-houses. The gunpowder was then milled, dried, granulated, polished, packed and transported in barrels, either by cart or by barge. Dartford's citizens unsurprisingly objected to the conveyance of gunpowder through the streets of the town, and in 1796 a new road was built to carry the powder to the storage site.

The Dartford mills were surrounded by large earthen embankments to minimise the damaging effects of accidental explosions, which were a regular feature on the site. In the 1790s alone, three separate explosions killed twenty-four workers and in 1833 at least sixteen separate detonations destroyed several mills, damaged buildings in the town and killed eight workers and several horses.

Precautions were taken to minimise the risks and impact. Workers wore slippers, not shoes, hand sewn with no metal; hinges, cogs and axles were oiled to avoid friction and sparks; even wheelbarrow wheels were rimmed with copper instead of iron.

The wars of the eighteenth century were economically beneficial to Kent, but the cost in terms of the lives and limbs of soldiers and sailors was high.

GREENWICH HOSPITAL—THE PORTICO

The King Charles Building at the Royal Hospital for Seamen at Greenwich has a portico of the Corinthian order, crowned with an entablature and pediment. In the pediment is a sculpture representing Fortitude and the Dominion of the Sea. (Author's collection)

It was to care for the latter that the royal palace at Greenwich was remodeled as a naval hospital to provide a counterpart for the Chelsea Hospital for soldiers. Sir Christopher Wren and his assistant Nicholas Hawksmoor gave their services free of charge as architects, and the work was completed by Sir John Vanbrugh to Wren's original plans. The building work was imaginatively funded. It used £19,500 in fines paid by merchants convicted of smuggling, a public fundraising appeal which brought in £9,000, and in 1705, an additional £6,472 comprising the liquidated value of estates belonging to the recently hanged pirate, Captain Kidd.

The hospital, although it had an infirmary, was designed primarily to accommodate pensioned sailors. The Great Hall was gorgeously decorated with murals extolling the many virtues of Queen Mary, its founder, and her husband King William. The hospital's oldest inmate is also depicted. John Wall, reputedly 97 years old, is shown as a venerable and worthy recipient of charity. In fact, he was an unreformed reprobate, always in trouble with the authorities for drunkenness and use of execrable naval language.

The smuggling merchants who were fined to fund the hospital building were only the unlucky ones who got caught, the tip of the criminal iceberg. By the eighteenth century, smuggling in Kent was at its peak as an alternative, and often very unsavoury, trade opportunity.

Earlier, the focus of the smugglers had been getting wool out of the country, rather than importing goods, although that could be an attractive sideline. For centuries England's chief raw material was wool. It was exported, after payment of duty, to Flanders particularly, where it fetched a good price, and was prized for its texture and length of staple. Wool smuggling, known as 'owling', grew up to avoid paying the export duty. The word owling is variously explained as coming from the hooting noise the smugglers used to warn of danger or as being a corruption of 'wooling'. Or perhaps it was because the smugglers worked at night.

Then, in 1614, James I issued a proclamation banning the export of wool. The measure was intended to halt the growth of the Flemish textile industries and promote the growth of domestic, especially Irish, enterprises. In Kent the export ban was a disaster. The loss of revenue could not be made up by sales to the domestic market. In 1703, it was reckoned that wool in its raw state was worth fourpence a pound in Ireland, and combed wool, tenpence. In France a seller could get two shillings and sixpence for raw wool and up to six shillings a pound for combed wool. Apart from the inconvenient fact that it was against the law, the argument for smuggling was very persuasive.

The owlers' enemies were the customs men. Until 1671, the normal method of customs duty collecting was 'farming'. An individual would pay a fixed sum to the Crown, and then collect customs duties in a given area and keep them. 'Farmers' appointed their own officials at ports. Alas, neither the farmers nor the officials were always honest men.

The special freedoms given to the Cinque Ports may have encouraged smuggling. The ports were able to apprehend and punish their own offenders and probably a blind eye was often turned to what was regarded as a legitimate means of supplementing a meagre income when times were hard (which they often were). If the choice for the authorities was to be between ignoring the fact that a man was a smuggler, and having him and his family as a charge on the parish, then pragmatism would surely win the day.

Arranging a ship, and men, to smuggle wool overseas involved a large financial outlay, with the possibility of great returns, and the men who bankrolled this were not averse to using violence if their plans were threatened. Punishment for smuggling was death if the culprit resisted; if not, he could expect to be transported or sent for navy service, neither of which was a desirable outcome. Threats were an effective way of ensuring the community's silence.

In 1601, a Star Chamber case against Ambrose Warde, gentleman, revealed some details he would rather have kept private. These included the allegation that he was a murderer who had acquired a royal pardon for 'a great sum of money' and that he was using his father's position as Captain of Sandgate Castle to facilitate an extensive smuggling operation. He used the barn at the castle to store 'great quantities' of wool, leather, tallow, corn, and most seriously munitions, which were shipped illegally overseas. He had beaten and severely injured one of the officers at the castle who threatened to betray him and threatened a fisherman, who became suspicious of his night-time activity, with the press gang.

Warde naturally denied the allegations and the fisherman who reported his activity later unaccountably withdrew his statement. No charges were brought.

The customs men were not above suspicion, either. In 1622, John Browning was accused of offering to smuggle some wool to France for Simon Head of Alkham. He told Head that he could get him six shillings a quarter, which is what he had got when he smuggled and sold his own wool. Browning was, at the time, the local customs officer. When the charge was investigated, the witnesses all realised that they had been mistaken, and the case was dropped.

When they did try to enforce the law, things could get nasty for the customs men. William Sneath, a customs collector, spotted a sloop approaching the shore at Shorncliffe one night in 1657. It was not a usual landing place and he suspected smuggling. He tried to seize the goods being landed, but was set upon by the recipients, about twelve men armed with staves. They had come ready for trouble. Both his assistants were injured in the fight, although one of them, armed with only a small 'fowling piece', tried to scare off their assailants.

Thirteen years later, it was the Mayor of Hythe who was implicated in criminality. When a smuggler was killed by a customs official early in 1685, Julius Deedes falsified evidence against the officer at the inquest. Knowing that he was liable to be arrested, he took advantage of a providential parliamentary election in Hythe and secured a seat. With it came parliamentary privilege against charges. The electorate was made up of the mayor and corporation of Hythe, and Deedes not only voted for himself in the election, but as mayor was also the returning officer. His plan backfired when his election was declared invalid, he was forced to resign as mayor, and most humiliatingly of all, the Lord High Steward of England vetoed his nomination as one of the canopy bearers at the coronation of James II.

Deedes bounced back and was re-elected to Parliament in 1689 and allowed to take part in the coronation of William and Mary, but his new-found respectability was short-lived. In May 1692, fourteen of his employees were arrested for a serious assault on customs officers who had seized wool from a barn belonging to Deedes, which they said were destined to be smuggled. The Customs Board said that it had been a legal seizure, based on 'reasonable suspicion'. Deedes said the customs men were acting illegally, as they had no constable with them as the law required, which was a little disingenuous of him as the said constable, Birch, was one of the men assaulting the customs officers and was in his pay. Deedes himself, at the time of the attack, was conveniently at home, 19 miles away, but Birch had incriminated him by showing his written order to some men at Lydd.

The situation looked bleak for Deedes, but he was saved once again from prosecution, this time by dying, in September 1692. He was something of a blot on the escutcheon of an otherwise unimpeachably respectable family.

The government had set up the national Customs Board in 1671 to try to combat smuggling more effectively. Sloops patrolled the south coast in search of the smugglers, but then fell foul of some seventeenth-century austerity measures and were replaced by locally employed riding officers, thus saving thousands of pounds a year. The result was that smuggling increased. Troops of dragoons were deployed to the ports and in desperation the government passed the Wool Act in 1698, forbidding anyone living within 15 miles of the coast from selling wool without a certificate from the Customs House. This desperate piece of legislation was as ineffective as all the other efforts had been.

By this time, smuggling imported goods, which were subject to Customs and Excise duties, had also become lucrative. The government used the duty raised to fund the never-ending wars, and the list of taxed items was endless too. Luxury goods such as wine, silk, lace, glass and china together with prosaic commodities such as salt, pepper, playing cards, spices, coffee and chocolate were subject to duty and were therefore smuggled. Tea was an especial favourite with smugglers during the eighteenth century because it was cheap to buy, easy to handle and had a ready market.

Smuggling was most easily arranged through loose organisations, the gangs. They had a justified reputation for violence and often succeeded through a reign of terror.

The Hawkhurst Gang are first heard of in 1740, attacking a group of dragoons led by a customs riding officer, Thomas Carswell. He had just found and seized some tea the Hawkhurst men had hidden in a barn. Carswell was shot dead. A little later, Richard Hawkins, a farm labourer suspected of stealing two bags of the gang's tea, was beaten and whipped to death and his body thrown in the village pond.

The gang extended its operations eastward into Sussex and Dorset. In 1747, near Chichester, they seized two customs officers who were on their trail. One was buried alive in a fox earth. The other, after being chained to an outhouse for several days was thrown down a well and stoned to death.

The now peaceful village of Hawkhurst remembers its violent past. (Anne Thompson)

The murderous brutality of the gang eventually alienated the people who had previously been happy to turn a blind eye to their exploits. At Goudhurst, the townsfolk formed the Goudhurst Band of Militia to prevent them coming into the town. In response, the Hawkhurst gang threatened to burn the town and kill the residents. When they carried out their threats and attacked, the militia were well enough trained to shoot dead three smugglers and force the withdrawal of the rest.

The next year, 1748, the government offered substantial rewards for the capture of gang members. The public were sufficiently sickened by the violence to oblige and the leaders were arrested, tried, and in several cases executed. The bodies of two of the leaders, Thomas Kingsmill and William Fairall were sent from Tyburn to Kent, to be hung in chains while they rotted.

The trials broke up the Hawkhurst Gang, but the lure of potentially huge profits encouraged others to spring up. Deal men were well known for their skill both as boat builders and as seamen, and a good few for their rapid cross-Channel trips. Their so-called centipede boats could make the crossing in two hours. The return trip, with a laden boat, was likely to have been slower. Their notoriety reached such a pitch that in 1781 the government acted. Hundreds of mounted soldiers and infantrymen descended on the town, but the Deal men had been tipped off, and managed to send most of what they had hidden back to France for safekeeping. The troops tried again three years later and this time, in front of the horrified eyes of the townspeople, burnt all their boats on the beach. They were not long deterred, and smuggling soon re-established itself as one of the main local industries until well into the nineteenth century.

In the north of the county, smuggling thrived in Gravesend, Cooling, Wrotham and the Hoo peninsula. One of the more successful gangs operated out of the quiet fishing village of Seasalter, where the group leased a farmhouse. One of its members, William Baldock, died with an extraordinary fortune of well over £1 million, perhaps because of his excellent local connections: his nephew was the local customs riding officer.

The government finally decided that only a military-style operation would defeat the smugglers, and under the leadership of Captain William McCulloch the Royal Naval Coast Blockade for the Patrolling of Smuggling was created in 1817. McCulloch's reputation as a disciplinarian is implicit

The Walnut Tree Inn in Aldington, where, it is said, a small window on the south of the building was used as a secret signalling point. (Anne Thompson)

in his nickname, 'Flogging Joey'. Sailing frigates, the captain's men patrolled the coast from Sheppey to Selsey Bill. Frequent shore parties went into towns to gather intelligence and keep watch. Bases were established at Deal and Hythe and a string of signalling stations was set up to link Deal with Beachy Head.

An organised approach was essential to deal with the highly effective Aldington Gang, smugglers, or Free Traders as they preferred to call themselves, from the Romney Marsh. They were organised, successful and very violent. Their HQ was at the Walnut Tree Inn in Aldington.

They had been active since about 1817, but the first opportunity the Blockade men had to confront them was at the 'Battle of Brookland' in 1821. They intercepted gang members offloading contraband on Camber Beach, and pursued them across the Marsh towards Brookland. Musket fire was exchanged and the Blockade men made repeated cutlass charges. Nine Blockade men were wounded, along with a dozen smugglers, and four of the Aldington Gang were killed and two captured. One, Cephas Quested, was subsequently hanged.

After Brookland, the leadership of the gang passed to George Ransley. In 1826, the gang was caught on the beach at Dover and killed a Blockade midshipman. A reward of £500 was offered for information which would lead to the murderers and, in October that year, a Deal man named them. They were arrested by Bow Street Runners in Aldington, tried and condemned to death, although their sentences were commuted to transportation. George Ransley was sent to Tasmania, where he was later joined by his wife and ten children. After he had been freed, he settled down to life as a successful and prosperous farmer.

The smuggling did not stop entirely, but the Blockade had served its purpose: this was the last time that a smuggling gang stood trial for taking up arms in Kent. The Blockade was wound up in 1831 and the coastguard took over its duties.

The end of the eighteenth century saw Britain at war with France again, but this time their army was led by a man determined to invade England and avenge his country for 'six hundred years of insult' – Napoleon Bonaparte. Building on plans developed by the *ancien regime*, he started as early as 1798 to plot his retribution, choosing Boulogne as his centre of operations and

This Doric-style temple was erected in Mote Park, Maidstone, by the Volunteers of Kent to commemorate the occasion of their 1799 royal review, and as a tribute to the Earl of Romney, who was Lord Lieutenant. (Anne Thompson)

reconnoitring the coast between Folkestone and Rye for suitable landing places. The Vicar of Lyminge, only 8km from the coast, chillingly warned his flock that 'before next Sunday dawns upon us, we might cease to be an independent nation'.

Had Napoleon invaded at this time, the Kent resistance would have comprised almost entirely the militias. The government had, in 1794, passed the Volunteer Act, calling for men to enrol, and the response in Kent had been enthusiastic. Those who could afford to own horses joined the East Kent or West Kent Yeomanry or, for 'spirited young men' only, the New Romney Fencible Cavalry. The less well-off joined the Volunteer units formed in most towns and cities, though New Romney, Lydd, Hythe and Folkestone pulled together as the Cinque Port Volunteers.

In 1799, the Lord Lieutenant of Kent, Lord Romney, invited the royal family, the Prime Minister William Pitt and 5,000 of the Yeomanry and Volunteers to a review in Mote Park, at Maidstone. The Volunteers wore oak leaves in their caps, a reminder of their forebears' fabled meeting with William the Conqueror, which gave rise to the county's motto *Invicta*. The king and queen watched marching, counter-marching, firing, salutes, and bands before a splendid dinner and a twenty-one-gun salute. The king, George III, said that the Kent militia had the 'virtues & manners which distinguish the genuine character of Englishmen'.

Napoleon's attention was briefly diverted from invading Britain when he was called to Egypt. He staged a coup d'état in France on his return and was named First Consul of the Republic and later, in 1804, Emperor of France. Domestic politics dealt with, he again turned his attentions across the Channel.

In Kent, preparations for this possibility had already started. The threat was real, and inspired the young Wordsworth to write:

VANGUARD of Liberty, ye men of Kent,
Ye children of a Soil that doth advance
Her haughty brow against the coast of France,
Now is the time to prove your hardiment!

Dover was seen as particularly vulnerable, because it offered a good harbour and a short sea crossing from France – it was the perfect landing place for the enemy. Work started with the castle. Two hundred guns were mounted in the castle ditch; many more were placed on the towers and curtain wall; the medieval keep was used as a powder magazine and its roof replaced by an explosive-proof brick vault. Outside the castle, massive bastions were built.

At the Western Heights, on the other side of the Dour Valley, two forts and two bastions linked together by a series of dry moats, encompassing barracks and a church, were constructed. Two detached forts completed the defences. The Grand Shaft inside the main complex gave access directly to the beach below. It is a triple spiral staircase built through the cliff which took three years to build. Once complete, it was tested. An entire regiment descended and assembled in Dover's market square, to the great consternation of the townsfolk, who had not been pre-warned of the exercise.

Two other forts were built at vulnerable spots in Dover, which meant that the town was as well defended as it could be, but had the effect of displacing the threat of invasion to the rest of the coast. To address this, simple, sturdy squat towers – the Martello towers – were built at regular intervals along the shoreline, at the most obvious landing places, with gun emplacements on top. The idea was proposed in 1803, inspired by a round fortress at Mortella Point in Corsica, but the procrastination of government meant that construction did not start until 1805, by which time Napoleon had been distracted by Austria, and Nelson's victory at Trafalgar meant that the invasion threat was over. However, the great machinery of the army and the government was unstoppable and the building works were completed in 1808 – seventy-three towers along the south coast.

Ten metres high, with only one entrance high up on the landward side, they were built to withstand whatever the enemy could throw at them. Each tower incorporated half a million bricks laid with hot lime mortar, which when set was as hard as iron. The towers were numbered, starting with No. 1 on the East Cliff at Folkestone and, in Kent, ending with No. 28 at St Mary's Bay. None of them was ever employed to repel an invasion.

At the same time that the Martello towers were being built, another defensive mechanism was being dug: the Royal Military Canal. Dungeness

Martello tower No. 1 stands 61m above the East Wear Bay in Folkestone. It is one of only twenty-six still standing. (Anne Thompson)

had been identified as another potential French landing place. Although there was no harbour, it was flat and sparsely populated. The first solution offered to this weakness was to flood the whole of the Romney Marsh when an invasion was imminent. Most of the land was below sea-level, but the plan was dependant on the state of the tide at the critical moment. Instead, the idea of a canal separating the marsh from the higher ground to the north was proposed, and work started in 1804. The canal was to run from Seabrook, near Folkestone to Hastings, a distance of 45km. It was not as simple a job as the plans had made it appear. After a bad experience with less-than-ideal private contractors, the army took over management of the works, employing over 1,000 workers from all over the country. The canal was not complete by the time the invasion threat had disappeared but, as with the Martello towers, the army took an 'I've started so I'll finish' approach and carried on regardless. The Kent section, 29km of it, was completed by 1806, and a couple of royal princes marked the occasion by taking a boat trip along its length.

The canal was never used for its intended purpose. It cost well over a quarter of a million pounds to build and became an embarrassing white elephant to the government. Desperate to recoup some of the cost, they opened it to navigation in 1807 and collected tolls for the transportation of produce and goods. There was even a regular passenger barge service running between Hythe and Rye, which took around four hours to complete. The Coastguard tried to use the canal to stop smuggling across the Marsh by putting guardhouses at each bridge along its length, but the guards proved easily bribable.

At the other end of the county, the Chatham Dockyard was vulnerable, not from the sea, where almost impenetrable defences already existed, but from an overland approach from a beachhead established elsewhere. To deal with this the Chatham lines were dug. Ditches, 8m wide and 2.5m deep, were excavated across a 2km stretch of open ground, and lined with brick. Magazines and bastions were created along their length. The main stronghold was Fort Amherst, still standing and now restored.

A peaceful stretch of the Royal Military Canal near Aldington. (Anne Thompson)

In 1802, Major-General John Moore, injured fighting Napoleon in Egypt and in need of rest and recuperation, was given command of the army in Kent. He had a vision of raising an elite brigade of light infantry, and the following year was appointed Colonel of the 52nd Regiment of Foot and given permission to train it as a light corps at Shorncliffe, near Folkestone. In their green jackets and trousers, they became a familiar sight in the surrounding area, and trained repelling invaders by wading chest high into the sea at Sandgate. Moore also made sure his troops were well housed and fed properly, earning himself a reputation as a comparatively humane commander. The barracks at Shorncliffe are named for him. In 1804, he was knighted, and three years later sent to Portugal and Spain to support resistance to the French there. Trying to save his army from Napoleon, he was killed at the Battle of Corunna in 1809.

The memorial to Sir John Moore at Sandgate, near the Shorncliffe barracks which still bear his name. (Anne Thompson)

Wellington's dispatch telling of his victory at Waterloo in 1815 was brought ashore at Broadstairs and travelled by post-chaise via Canterbury, Sittingbourne, Rochester and Blackheath to London. It was the end, at last, of war with France. Despite the millions of pounds spent on fortifications and defences in Kent, Napoleon was defeated off the coast of Spain by Nelson and in Belgium by Wellington. Like Hitler, he could have attacked Britain, and may well have won, but he chose not to.

The Royal Military Canal is now the setting for a biennial Venetian fete in Hythe and provides good fishing for anglers and an abundance of bird-life for twitchers. The Grand Shaft in Dover was used for pedestrian access to the town of Dover and was segregated by rank: one staircase for 'officers and their ladies', one for 'sergeants and their wives' and the third for 'soldiers and their women'. Wildflowers grow across the Chatham Lines. The Martello towers, too robust to be demolished, remained at their posts. Some gently rotted away; some were converted to dwelling houses; some were used as signal relay stations; one was painted by Turner; others were put to use by the Coastguard in the war against smuggling; and one is a tourist attraction in Dymchurch.

Kent had prospered from the wars of the eighteenth century, but after Waterloo had to readjust to peace for the first time in over twenty years.

Seven

THE TOWNS

T he eighteenth and nineteenth centuries were a time of huge urban expansion throughout the country, and Kent was no exception. In 1700, none of the county's towns had more than 10,000 residents, but fifty years later there were fifteen and Greenwich, the largest, had a population of 35,000.

The other big urban centres were mostly country towns, with markets and shops serving the surrounding rural area, trading with other towns, especially London, and often on a navigable river, like Maidstone. Their growth was enabled by the development of a county-wide communications network which grew at an astonishing rate, fuelled by a succession of national 'manias' for new types of transport.

The first to strike, after a slow start, was turnpike mania. Since the 1660s, it had been possible for groups of local entrepreneurs to band together to establish Turnpike Trusts by Act of Parliament. The concept was simple: the consortium improved roads, made them suitable for wheeled traffic and maintained them and in exchange could set up toll gates and charge road users. Although the businessmen could not directly profit, they would benefit from improved trade links.

The idea was slow to catch on, and the first Kent Turnpike Act was not until 1709, for the Sevenoaks to Tonbridge road. Then sections of Watling Street, the route from London to the cross-Channel port of Dover, got attention, followed by the road from London to Tunbridge Wells, Kent's fashionable answer to Bath Spa. The road from Canterbury to Whitstable was next in 1736, improving the city's links to the coast and London.

But in the mid-eighteenth century the nation was seized with turnpike mania, and in the twenty years after 1751 more than 18,500 miles of

The Toll Cottage in Nonington stood beside the toll gate in the village. (Anne Thompson)

English road were turnpiked. Twenty-two new trusts were established in Kent, producing a network between the towns and villages of the Weald and Maidstone. The east of the county caught up later, with the tolling of roads fanning out of Canterbury, improving links with the coastal towns. Despite their obvious advantages, the turnpikes were not always welcomed: in 1766, the inhabitants of Maidstone objected strongly to having to pay to use roads which had previously been free, and demanded that no tollgate should be situated within half a mile of the town. Their complaints were ignored.

In the 1790s, turnpike mania in Kent was replaced by canal mania, following the huge commercial success of the canals built in the North of England to carry coal. Although there was considerable enthusiasm for the idea in the county, there was actually very little trade imperative to dig canals in an area so well served by its coastline and navigable rivers.

Notwithstanding the lack of actual need, there were several schemes to build Kent canals. The first was to link Canterbury by canal to the coast.

In 1797 a canal to Reculver was proposed, in 1810 another to St Nicholas Bay near Margate, and in 1824 another to Sandwich. None managed to secure adequate financial backing. Then there were plans to link the rivers Thames and Medway with the River Rother to make a through waterway from London to Rye harbour. A plan was drawn up, a committee of wealthy businessmen organised and the plan approved by Parliament. The proposed canal would carry chalk, lime and coal into the Weald and timber and agricultural produce out of it. The businessmen then realised that the likely traffic would be too low to produce a healthy income from tolls, and withdrew their investment. The plan languished, raising its head occasionally, but always failing to get proper backing, and was finally allowed to die in 1815.

The only canal actually built in Kent was the Thames and Medway Canal, which was not an unqualified success. The canal was first mooted in 1778 as a shortcut for military craft from Deptford and Woolwich on the Thames to Chatham Dockyard on the Medway, avoiding the 74km journey around the peninsula and through the Thames estuary. It would also carry commercial traffic between the two rivers.

Planning did not start until 1799 and digging began the next year, but costs escalated, the route was altered and a tunnel had to be dug. By the time it opened, no less than twenty-four years later, the canal had required five Acts of Parliament and cost over £260,000. However, the tunnel between Strood and Higham was considered one of the engineering triumphs of the age. Three and a half kilometres long, dug through chalk by hand, it was apparently wide enough and tall enough to accommodate a 61-tonne sailing barge with its mast lowered. It is unlikely that it ever had to. In 1846, the canal company sold the tunnel to the South Eastern Railway Company, which filled in the canal and laid a double railway track over it.

Railway mania was the third and last of the transport crazes. The impact of rail technology in the nineteenth century was so far-reaching that it is comparable to the development of the internet, opening up previously unimaginable opportunities for trade and communications.

The first railway in the South of England was the line from Canterbury to Whitstable, which opened in 1830. Until then, Canterbury's main line of supply for goods had been along the River Stour from Ramsgate on the coast. Although this is only 27km as the crow flies, the meandering river journey is four times as long and the river was continually silting up. Whitstable, on the coast about 11km north, was a small fishing village and port and ideal, except that it was about 60m lower than Canterbury and had no proper harbour.

The complicated construction work, under the direction of the pioneering George Stephenson, took two years, and the building of Whitstable harbour, overseen by Thomas Telford, was completed in 1832. From the beginning, the Canterbury and Whitstable Railway was a public service, intended for passengers as well as freight. The world's first rail season ticket was issued for use on the line in 1834, to take Canterbury passengers to the Whitstable beaches for the summer season. The railway coaches apparently bore the insignia 'C&W' for Canterbury and Whitstable, but local wags renamed it the Crab and Winkle line.

The line used cable haulage by stationary steam engines over much of its length, with locomotives restricted to the short level stretch. It was never a financial success, but staggered on under various owners until 1952, when it closed.

Part of the trackway of the old Crab and Winkle railway line has now been reopened as a cycle way and footpath from Canterbury to Whitstable. (Anne Thompson)

Other railway lines, more successful, followed. At first, a host of small companies opened short stretches of line. In 1845, the Gravesend and Rochester Railway opened a line linking Gravesend with Strood. In 1860, the East Kent Railway opened a line from Strood to Canterbury which was extended to Dover. Margate and Ramsgate were linked to Herne Bay, Faversham and Ashford; Sittingbourne and Sheerness were linked; so were Tonbridge and Tunbridge Wells.

Then the South Eastern Railway (SER) emerged as one of the big players in the game, and in 1845 connected Dover to Folkestone and Ashford and thence to London. The impact on cross-Channel traffic was huge.

Dover had until then a near-monopoly on ferry crossings to France, using the port of Calais, but in 1843, when the railway reached the edge of Folkestone, the SER bought the town's choked and nearly derelict harbour. They dredged it, and the New Commercial Steam Packet Company was subcontracted to provide a ferry service to Boulogne. A steeply graded branch line from Folkestone town station down to the harbour was constructed and when, on the French side of the Channel, the railway reached Boulogne, it was possible to travel from London to Paris in a record fourteen hours. The railway company also invested in Dover, and by 1848 the SER provided two steam ships a day between Folkestone and Boulogne, one a day between Dover and Calais, and one between Dover and Ostend.

Alone of the Cinque Ports, Dover had survived with a viable harbour. Its Roman harbour, which was navigable into what is now the town centre, silted up, and was relocated in an area beneath the castle. This was abandoned in its turn in 1370, in favour of a site to the west of the town, but silting continued, and several piers were built and abandoned or destroyed. In 1583, Thomas Digges, an engineer championed by Sir Walter Raleigh, proposed confining sea water in a large pent, or reservoir at high tide and releasing it at low water to clear the harbour entrance of shingle. Despite some setbacks, the system worked, and in 1606 James I took ownership away from Dover Corporation and gave the harbour its own charter under the leadership of the Lord Warden of the Cinque Ports and 'eleven discreet men'. This new organisation was the forerunner of Dover Harbour Board which still manages the port today.

Improvements to the port were made throughout the seventeenth and eighteenth centuries, but cross-Channel travel was still an uncertain undertaking. The crossing time was about five hours, and passengers arriving at the tidal harbour at low water had to be landed on the beach by small boat, an unpleasant and invariably damp experience. In 1625, for the arrival of Charles I's bride Henrietta Maria, a moveable bridge was built to avoid such a possibility. The young princess, terribly seasick after a ten-hour crossing, had to be carried up to Dover Castle in a litter.

When the railway arrived in 1844, the harbour was increased in size by a further 2 hectares. At the same time the Admiralty proposed Dover as a port of refuge for large warships, to fill the lack of any other safe harbour between Portsmouth and Chatham. Work on the Admiralty Pier, the first stage of the development, started in 1848, and although the harbour

In 1853, the SER opened the Lord Warden Hotel near the Admiralty Pier where the ferries berthed. It attracted a clientele from rich and famous travellers, including Dickens, Thackeray and the Emperor Napoleon III. (Anne Thompson)

of refuge was slow to develop (the work took fifty years), cross-Channel steamers used the pier to embark and disembark passengers. In the 1860s, trains started to run along the pier, delivering passengers almost to the gangplanks of the new steamships which now carried cross-Channel traffic.

The coming of the South Eastern Railway impacted significantly on the town of Ashford, too. Until the mid-1840s it had been a small country settlement of about 3,000 souls, with a monthly stock market and the usual range of rural occupations. Its expansion was limited by the lack of a navigable river for water transport of freight. Toll roads had improved the situation a little, but carriers still struggled with heavy goods. In 1836, Samuel Steddy, an Ashford timber merchant, gave evidence to a parliamentary committee that he was quite unable to meet the demand for timber from London, particularly in winter when the roads were in a bad state. The landlord of the Saracen's Head in the town complained about the cost of transporting spirits and porter, as well as coal, all brought from Faversham in his own wagons. A butcher, a grocer and an ironmonger had similar complaints. The town welcomed the railway with open arms

Ashford station opened on 1 December 1842. By 1850 the lines to Dover, Folkestone and Hastings were all in use. The working life of the town was transformed, with an influx of skilled workers, new businesses and even regional commuters to the town, but the decision by the SER to site their main works at Ashford had an even greater effect. Ashford locomotive works was built in 1847 on a new 75-hectare site, and by 1850 130 houses had been built for the workers in an area called Alfred Town by the company, but New Town by everyone else. The cottages were two-storey flats built around a green, with a public house. The high quality of the housing, compared to the hovels of the poor, or even the housing of local agricultural workers, encouraged inward migration. The works employed about 600 people in 1850 and over 900 ten years later, and the company opened a carriage and wagon works on an adjacent 13-hectare site.

In the north of the county, the London and Greenwich Railway, built between 1836 and 1837, made daily commuting from Kent to London a real possibility. Its terminus was London Bridge station, the first major railway terminus to be built in London. To avoid wholesale demolition work and countless level crossings, the railway was imaginatively built on a viaduct.

The SER provided a public house, the Alfred Arms, for its workers on the green at New Town, Ashord. Its doors are still open today. (Anne Thompson)

Small roads could simply pass under the arches of the viaduct, while larger roads and canals along the way could have specially constructed bridges going over them. This new use of the viaduct, as a way of running a railway line into a city without blocking roads, was unique, and proved to be a solution that would be copied in countless cities around the world.

Some 400 workmen were employed to build the railway, laying about 100,000 bricks a day. The viaduct towered over the landscape in an astonishing line of 851 arches and twenty-seven bridges, majestically cutting a path through the fields, orchards and market gardens of Kent and the factories and slums of south-east London. It remains today the longest railway viaduct in Britain. It was not just functional but was designed to be beautiful as well, complete with fine red and yellow brickwork, gas lighting along the full length, and a boulevard alongside planted with trees so that, for the charge of a penny, people could walk along as though down a splendid Victorian street.

It was planned from the beginning that the spaces under the arches would be let as workshops, a tradition that has continued to the present day. Plans to use them for housing were unrealistic, as the arches were damp and, inevitably, noisy.

The huge quantity of bricks used in building the viaduct came from Faversham, brought to Deptford Creek by sailing barge. The job made the reputation of the local product, and more and more brickfields opened in the area, until Faversham was virtually encircled by fourteen of them. The dramatic growth of Victorian London was founded on Kent brick.

The London developers favoured yellow, rather than red bricks. Brickworks in Faversham and Sittingbourne produced these by mixing the local high-quality brick earth with chalk, also readily available locally, to produce their yellow 'London stocks'. In a refinement of the process, they started adding coal ash to the mixture, producing a brick which could be fired without the need for a kiln. The 'green' bricks were set in huge piles, and kindling lit beneath them. The ash still had enough energy left in it to burn and bake the bricks.

The barges which delivered the bricks to quays and wharves in London returned to Kent laden with domestic refuse, bought from local authorities for a farthing a ton. The cargo was sifted for ash for use in the brickworks and the residue used to strengthen sea defences in the Swale estuary. While apparently an ecologically sound enterprise, working conditions were appalling. The sifting was filthy work, carried out mainly by women and children for miserable pay. The bricks were all made by hand, and the employees were paid piecework rates. A man needed to make 50,000 bricks a week, although very few could, to make a reasonable wage, and the labour was literally sweated in the heat of the firing process. There was no hope of getting better-paid work, as the brickfield owners operated a cartel to ensure that wages did not vary from field to field. Manufacturing was only possible from April to September and other work was hard to come by, except digging the brick earth in winter.

Brick was also needed in the building boom in the expanding Kent towns. Those who profited from the growth of trade and wealth in towns started to build themselves new houses in what we think of today as 'Georgian' style. Built of brick, the houses were characterised by

This street in Sandwich has a medieval house which has been updated with Georgian windows, an original hall house, and, behind them, tall new-build Georgian houses. (Anne Thompson)

proportion and balance. Mathematical ratios were used to determine the height of a window in relation to its width or the shape of a room as a double cube. If you could not afford to build a new house, you could modernise by adding a whole new brick front to your timber-framed house, or cover your old facade with tiles or weatherboarding, depending on where you lived. Weatherboarding was particularly favoured in the Weald and around Tenterden. In Canterbury and Sandwich, where economic growth had been less dramatic, the cheaper option of plastering over a timber frame was favoured and older small windows were replaced with large Georgian ones.

Not all urban expansion can be attributed solely to improved communications. Other influences came into play. One of these was the threat to the coast during the Napoleonic Wars which changed the character of those towns where troops were stationed, and nowhere more than at the coastal towns of Sandgate, Hythe and Folkestone.

Sandgate, a quiet village between Folkestone and Hythe, had tolerated until 1798 the annual round of militia training at Shorncliffe camp, but had not exerted itself to entertain the troops and boasted only one inn. Then the arrival of Sir John Moore, the establishment of Shorncliffe camp as a centre of excellence for the army and an influx of soldiers and visitors brought with them a seemingly inexhaustible demand for hospitality and services. Inns sprang up to suit every layer of the highly stratified military organisation, and there was a rash of house building. A newsroom was provided together with a library. Sandgate started to become a fashionable resort. Sir John Moore rented a house there for three guineas a week in winter, but complained it would be twice that in summer. There was, inevitably, some bad behaviour, but Sandgate Castle provided a convenient overnight lock-up for the inebriated.

Peaceful Hythe, with a population of fewer than 2,000, was swamped by the presence of 10,000 troops at the height of the Napoleonic Wars. Weatherboard accommodation and a temporary military hospital were built at the western end of the town and William Cobbett wrote that 'the hills are covered in barracks'. The officers and their ladies expected entertainment, and the town obliged by providing Assembly Rooms for dancing and card games in the new town hall on Friday evenings. A theatre was built and there, on Saturday nights, visitors could be entertained by a drama followed by renditions of such favourite songs of the time as 'The Widow Waddle of Chickabiddy Lane'. A box cost only three shillings.

The town saw the grim realities of war, too. After the Battle of Corunna in 1809, the returning troops were paraded at Hythe, but were in a sad state. Unceremoniously disembarked at Dover, they had been obliged to make their own way back to the town. The hospital was full of the dying and injured, and the presence of maimed soldiers in the town was a common sight. Sir John Moore did not return with his men. He was buried wrapped in his military cloak in the town ramparts at Corunna, dying after he heard that the French had lost the day.

For leisure purposes, ordinary soldiers found Folkestone more to their liking than Sandgate or Hythe, despite the fact that it was described in the early nineteenth century as being one of the most disagreeable towns in England, with 'muddy alleys instead of streets, and mean, poorly built houses'. There were plenty of public houses of the sort patronised by seafaring men, and the troops brought in some money, but also some crime. A soldier was convicted of rape and robbery in 1806, but most of the bad behaviour was confined to drunkenness and theft. When the invasion scare and the soldiers went away, the town declined again, but by 1830 it was starting to make efforts to attract fashionable people. Its sea bathing was described as good, but visitors were told to avoid the pig-sties, hovels and rookeries around the harbour.

Folkestone was trying to cash in on the fashion for sea bathing, and although it would not become a successful resort until much later in the nineteenth century, other Kent towns were already profiting from the vogue for visiting places whose only function was to provide curative waters and leisure facilities.

Royal Tunbridge Wells was the first town in England to develop purely as a resort. It was a remote place, of a few scattered cottages, not even a proper village until in 1606 Lord North, a fashionable but ailing courtier, passing through, drank from a spring there and on returning home found he was cured. It was clear to him that the waters had healed him, and he recommended the place to his friends. They also found the iron- and mineral-bearing water therapeutic, and the place began to develop a reputation. In 1630, Queen Henrietta Maria came to take the waters after giving birth to the future Charles II.

It was then still entirely rustic. Visitors, even Her Majesty, had to camp on common land as there were no lodging facilities, and its appeal lay partly in the opportunity it gave the urban rich to play at being simple country folk. Some basic facilities were built next to the spring in 1636, and thirty years later a hall was added for shelter in wet weather.

By then, Catherine of Braganza, the queen of Charles II, was a regular visitor, and the 1680s saw a building boom in the town. Plots alongside the 160m promenade near the springs were leased for the development of shops, places of refreshment or gaming houses. A colonnade was built in front of the row, which became known as The Pantiles. Tradesmen there dealt in the luxury goods demanded by their patrons, including Tunbridge ware, a kind of decoratively inlaid woodwork, and there were coffee houses and two gambling rooms, one for the lottery, another for the game of hazard. Lodging houses were built elsewhere in the town.

As Master of Ceremonies at Tunbridge Wells, 'Beau' Nash organised entertainments and established strict rules for correct behaviour. A notorious gambler, he died destitute and is buried in an unmarked pauper's grave in Bath. (Anne Thompson)

One early treatise on the waters, published by Dr Madan in 1687, said that they roused 'men and women to Amorous Emotions and Titillations'. The recommended dose of Tunbridge Wells water was one-and-a-half to two-and-a-half litres a day, and it is hardly surprising, if the claims for the water's aphrodisiac effects were true, that the town soon developed a reputation as the most scandalous of the spa resorts.

The advent of turnpike roads gave Tunbridge Wells easier access and on weekdays a public coach made nine return journeys between the town and London. During the eighteenth century its growth continued, as did its patronage by the wealthy leisured classes. Visits from the glitterati, among them Daniel Defoe, Fanny Burney, Tobias Smollet and Samuel Richardson, gave it celebrity cachet. In 1735, 'Beau' Nash, the leading light of the Bath social scene, appointed himself as Master of Ceremonies for Tunbridge Wells too. He remained in this position until his death in 1762, and under his patronage the town reached the height of its popularity as a fashionable resort.

The nineteenth century saw Tunbridge Wells settle into respectability and become the retirement destination of choice for retired officers and members of the colonial service. In 1909, Edward VII granted it the title 'Royal' in recognition of its long association with the monarchy. It is one of only three towns in the country to be so honoured. So ultra-respectable did the place become that by the twentieth century it had become the home of the mythical writer of outraged letters to the newspapers, 'Disgusted of Tunbridge Wells'.

Tunbridge Wells began to decline as a resort when sea bathing was taken up by the leisured classes as the latest fad. In the 1750s, Dr Richard Russell published an English translation of his Latin treatise A *Dissertation on the Use of Sea-Water in the Diseases of the Glands, Particularly the Scurvy, Jaundice, King's Evil, Leprosy, and the Glandular Consumption*. His work revolutionised the leisure pursuits of the country for centuries to come. Russell recommended bathing in sea water as a treatment for a huge range of diseases, and even drinking sea-water, in measured doses. This had, he said, cured 'strumous swellings', and 'scrophulous tumours'. At the same time, physicians began to extol the benefits of sea air, especially for anyone suffering from chest complaints.

These theories coincided with the growing popularity of the established spas with nouveau riche merchants. The new seaside resorts were more exclusive for those who wanted to escape from the vulgarity of the common herd. As a bonus, taking spa waters could have undesirable digestive after-effects, whereas sea bathing could be enjoyed in its own right.

Margate cashed in early on the trend, offering sea-bathing facilities from the 1730s. By 1769 it had a Master of Ceremonies, new purpose-built Assembly Rooms where there were dancing and games of whist, quadrille, commerce and loo, two circulating libraries and a bathing house. The bathing house formalised the process of sea bathing, which was not to be undertaken lightly. At Margate, one wrote one's name on a slate and waited for a bathing machine to become free. Pianofortes, newspapers and telescopes were provided in the waiting room. Bathing machines had been perfected by a Margate Quaker, Benjamin Beale. They were horse-drawn caravans, screened at both ends. Once a machine was available, the bather, fully dressed, climbed inside and undressed. Women, and sometimes men, changed into bathing costumes. Men were, however, allowed to bathe nude until 1860, when Victorian prudery prevailed. Once the machine had been driven into the sea, the driver operated a pulley and the front screen, which was rather like a hood, unfurled so that the bather could descend into the sea in complete privacy in a bath about 3.5ms long by 2m wide. It cost a shilling to hire a machine with a 'guide' to take it down to the water.

After bathing, a healthy walk was recommended. In 1763, a local guide suggested that people go onto the sands to collect pebbles, seashells and

After many vicissitudes, including use as a chapel, warehouse and bingo hall, the Theatre Royal at Margate once again offers a wide range of dramatic productions and shows. (Anne Thompson)

seaweed, with which, once dried, artistic creations could be fashioned and pasted into scrap books. The Margate sands were so extensive that in good weather it was possible to walk on them for six hours a day. At other times, an artificial rural pleasure garden, the Dandelion, could provide amusement.

The evenings offered a variety of entertainments. By 1762, a regular theatrical season was underway in a converted barn, and in 1785, Francis Cobb, a leading local brewer, built a new theatre for which, at great cost, he secured a royal charter enabling him to call it the Theatre Royal. In 1797, Mrs Jordan, actress and mistress of the future William IV, was paid £300 for performances for six nights in Garrick's *The Country Girl*.

The least expensive way to get from London to Margate before the railway came was by boat, a sailing packet at first, then later a steamboat. It may have been cheap, but it was often crowded and uncomfortable, too, and when the weather was bad, very unpleasant. The wealthy often sent their servants by this route and travelled themselves by carriage via Canterbury, or, by the end of the eighteenth century, direct. For the return journey, a diligence (horse-drawn coach) left Margate every morning at 4 a.m. and deposited its passengers in Piccadilly late that night for 1s 6d.

At the same time, the middle classes were starting to use the sea route, and the arrival of the railway made the destination even more popular. Margate could become very crowded as a result. Between 1817 and 1835 the steamboat traffic more than quadrupled, and in 1831 there were thought to have been up to 20,000 visitors. The town's summers were now dominated by the vulgar tradesman and his numerous family, and fashionable people started to look elsewhere.

Ramsgate briefly offered the cachet of royal patronage. Queen Victoria visited several times as a child with her mother the Duchess of Kent, and in 1821 George IV used the port to sail for Hanover in his yacht the *Royal George*. He had shunned Dover because the town, in a shocking breach of etiquette, had given a royal welcome to his rejected wife, Caroline, on her way to gate-crash the coronation. Ramsgate worthies made the most of the occasion. In honour of the king's visit, Ramsgate harbour was given the prefix 'Royal' and they erected an obelisk 'as a grateful record of his Majesty's gracious condescension in selecting this Port for his Embarkation on the 25th September in Progress to his Kingdom of Hanover and his happy Return on the 8th November 1821'.

The poet Coleridge regularly holidayed in Ramsgate, alone, as he had abandoned his wife and children in the Lake District. His first visit was in 1819, and he preferred to sea-bathe away from the crowds, walking out to Dumpton Gap between Ramsgate and Broadstairs. He recorded his experience in verse which cannot be said to be among his best:

Dismounting from my steed I'll stray
Beneath the cliffs of Dumpton Bay.
Where, Ramsgate and Broadstairs between,
Rude caves and grated doors are seen.
(From *The Delinquent Travellers*)

In between dips, he read Dante and Cicero and took opium.

In 1816, in a direct challenge to Margate, Ramsgate started to offer to the public warm sea-water baths in heated rooms. The rivalry between the two resorts resulted, by the 1840s, in bathing arrangements to suit every taste and purse: vapour baths, tubular baths, plunge baths, medicinal baths and, the very latest, *en douche* baths (showers) were all offered in one or both of the resorts.

The seaside resorts of Kent owed their initial expansion to demand for accommodation and services generated by transitory seekers of health and pleasure, but they also benefitted enormously from the revolutions in transport, and would continue to do so throughout the nineteenth century, and well into the twentieth. It was the next transport revolution, the availability of cheap air travel to sunnier beaches, which eventually led to their decline.

Improvements in transport also meant that, for the first time in history, one could live in the attractive Kent suburbs around London and commute into the city every day for work. Inevitably, the suburbs grew more populous, even crowded, until the boundaries between town and country were eroded. When the County of London was created in 1889, the Kent towns of Deptford, Greenwich, Woolwich, Lee, Eltham, Charlton, Kidbrooke and Lewisham were included in the new administrative area and officially became part of the great London sprawl.

Eight

'YE HAVE THE POOR ALWAYS WITH YOU'[1]

The population of Kent, and of the rest of England, continued to rise throughout the eighteenth and nineteenth centuries. Opinion is divided on whether this was because of lower mortality, increased fertility or a combination of both, but whatever the cause, the poor law system was stretched to breaking point and the situation was worsened by a series of economic depressions.

The law had not changed much since the sixteenth century. Each parish maintained its poor, funded through the poor rates, by providing cash, food or goods. There was a constant tension between those who wanted to reduce the rates and those who advocated a benevolent approach. Although the Elizabethan Poor Law Acts had made provision for workhouses, it was not until the end of the seventeenth century that the idea started to develop of supporting able-bodied labourers in this way. The idea at this time was to bring the workers and raw material together in one place so that the paupers could earn their keep.

An Act of 1722 put the idea to the test. It was sponsored by Sir Edward Knatchbull, a Kent baronet and MP, descended from generations of local gentry. Knatchbull's Act permitted groups of parishes to set up workhouses, minimising individual capital outlay, and to contract out or 'farm' the management of the place. The 'farmers', or subcontractors, were paid per workhouse inmate, usually about two shillings a week. Thus in Whitstable in 1770, the illiterate Richard Johnson was contracted to run

1 Mark, 14:7.

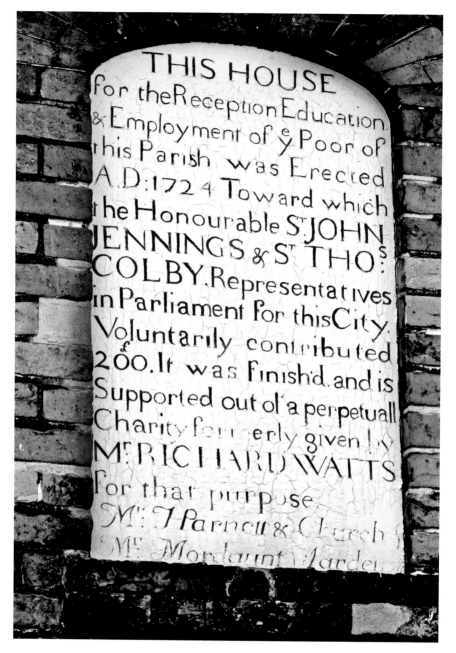

THIS HOUSE
for the Reception Education
& Employment of y̆ᵉ Poor of
this Parish was Erected
A.D: 1724 Toward which
the Honourable Sʳ JOHN
JENNINGS & Sʳ THOˢ:
COLBY. Representatives
in Parliament for this City.
Voluntarily contributed
£200. It was Finish'd. and is
Supported out of a perpetuall
Charity formerly given by
Mʳ RICHARD WATTS
for that purpose
Mʳ J Parnell & Church
Mʳ Mordaunt Warden

The plaque above the door of Rochester St Margaret's workhouse, erected under the auspices of Knatchbull's Act. Before the workhouse was opened, it was reckoned that the cost of maintaining the poor of the parish was 945 shillings a year, but the workhouse reduced the cost to the ratepayer to 574 shillings. (Anne Thompson) the workhouse and was given coal, hay for the workhouse cow, and two shillings per head for each pauper. He would also take a quarter of any profit their work made.

Knatchbull's Act workhouses were not always profitable. In Wye the inhabitants were put to spinning wool, but the costs of preparing the wool and paying an expert to train the paupers outweighed the profits. Chatham workhouse made a profit by investing almost nothing in raw materials, and set its seventy-odd paupers to work picking oakum, unravelling old tarry ropes for recycling at the shipyard. Just down the road at Rochester two smaller Knatchbull workhouses were built, and there, as at Chatham, the city authorities took the decision not to subcontract the management.

The former Wickhambreaux workhouse, now private houses. The little village near Canterbury was part of the Petham Gilbert union. (Anne Thompson)

The farming system was wide open to abuse, as the subcontractors made their profits from the sweated labour of the inmates and provision of substandard food and services. They were described at the time as 'the worst of tyrants', and one of Knatchbull's own kinsmen, John Toke, the squire of Godinton, near Ashford, said that they were like 'Egyptian Taskmasters', holding the inmates in terror. He proposed a plan for the management of Ashford workhouse based on his benevolent view that the aged, the sick and children should be well fed and clothed and made as comfortable as possible. His scheme was adopted.

As the eighteenth century drew on, there was an increasing feeling, locally and nationally, that such kindly administration was a cause of idleness in the poor. In 1786, an Ashford tradesman, a Mr Creed, recommended that the town should adopt a much more authoritarian approach. He wanted to prevent the poor leaving the workhouse without permission and to abolish support for illegitimate children over the age of 7, and for more than three children in a family. The surplus offspring were to be put into the workhouse without their parents. The compassionate John Toke refused to serve on the committee running the workhouse, but the vestry passed a vote of thanks to Mr Creed for introducing the system and reducing the burden on the town rates.

Another short-lived attempt at humanising the treatment of the poor resulted from Gilbert's Act of 1782, named for its sponsor Thomas Gilbert. It abolished the farming system, set up a regime of workhouse management by a Board of Guardians and included a list of standard rules under which workhouses were supposed to operate. In Kent, twelve Gilbert unions were formed, mostly in East Kent.

Gilbert's Act did nothing to reduce poor rates. It also allowed parishes to set up parish farms, intended to provide employment and be self-supporting, and a few Kent villages, such as Cranbrook, tried this, but without much success. They were rarely economically viable. The highest unemployment rate was in the winter when there was no work to be done on the parish farm. When work was needed, especially at harvest time, only the weakest or idlest were available.

As the eighteenth century turned into the nineteenth, attitudes to the poor started to harden. Relentless population growth produced a surplus of rural labour and underemployment, and after the end of the Napoleonic

wars, demobilisation followed by economic depression brought widespread unemployment.

The poor themselves blamed three groups of people for their plight: the parsons with their tithe system of taxation to support the Church; magistrates and poor law officers who withheld relief; and the rich tenant farmers who had been progressively lowering wages while introducing labour-saving agricultural machinery, particularly the horse-powered threshing machine which could do the work of many men. The disastrous harvest of 1829 did nothing to improve their mood.

On 30 August 1830, William Dodd, who farmed at Upper Hardres, near Canterbury, went before the city magistrates and asked for protection. He made a statement that during the previous week several threshing machines in the area had been broken, at Parmstead, Lyminge and Elham. The acts had been carried out by a 'riotous and tumultuous assembly of persons of the number of one hundred and upwards'. The Swing Riots had begun.

The name came from the signature on the letters sent to farmers, magistrates and parsons, 'Captain Swing', the mythical figurehead of the protesters' movement. 'Swing' was apparently a reference to the swinging of the flail used in hand threshing. The letters were first mentioned by *The Times* in October 1830, and threatened death or destruction of property. By the third week of October more than a hundred threshing machines had been destroyed in East Kent, and the riots spread across the country.

The Kent men who started it all were arrested and brought before the magistrates. They were harangued at length and told that they could be transported for seven years but then sentenced to three days' imprisonment. Sir Robert Peel, the Home Secretary, was furious, calling the sentence 'unparalleled leniency'. Thereafter, the full weight of the law was brought to bear on Swing rioters. Nationally, over 600 were jailed, 19 executed and over 500 transported. However, despite their slogan 'Bread or Blood', only one person is recorded as having been killed during the riots, and that was one of the rioters by the action of a soldier.

The riots added to the social, political and agricultural unrest throughout Britain in the 1830s, encouraging a wide demand for political reform. This included calls for harsher treatment of the poor, who, it was believed, were encouraged to be idle by the existing poor law system.

The Victorian workhouse of popular imagination, described by Dickens in *Oliver Twist*, was established by the 1834 Poor Law Amendment Act, which was in effect for nearly a century. It was based on the deterrence of pauperism and the complete abolition of outdoor relief in favour of concentrating provision on the workhouse, and was clear that the workhouse was to be as uninviting as possible. No one would want to enter voluntarily, and different classes of paupers would be segregated and families broken up.

There was opposition to the new law, particularly in the North of England. In Kent there were sporadic outbreaks of anti-poor law violence, principally in the Faversham area. Local poor law officials were manhandled, and their papers ripped to shreds at Bapchild; at Doddington they were assaulted and threatened by men with staves; at Rodmersham the military were called and arrests made. Meanwhile, at Chatham a group of disaffected paupers were threatened by soldiers with fixed bayonets.

The sign in the churchyard of St Michael's church, Hernhill, commemorating the dead of the Battle of Bossenden Wood. Two others were buried in Boughton. (Anne Thompson)

Discontent among the agricultural poor rumbled on until 1838, when on 31 May the self-styled Sir William Courtenay and nine of the labourers who followed him were killed by soldiers in the day-long Battle of Bossenden Wood. Courtenay was actually John Nichols Tom, a Truro malster who had spent four years in the Kent Lunatic Asylum. On his release, he espoused the cause of the poor, set himself up with a grey horse and carrying a flag atop a hop pole, he assembled a group of malcontent disciples in the Hernhill area. For some unknown misdemeanor, a warrant was issued for his arrest, but he shot and killed the constable sent to take him, provoking a military response. He and some of his followers are buried in Hernhill church.

The central body set up to administer the new workhouses system was the Poor Law Commission, which abolished Gilbert unions, and divided the country up into groups of parishes known as poor law unions. Every union had to set up a workhouse.

One of the earliest Poor Law Commissioners, Sir Francis Bond Head, was sent to Kent in 1834. A failed businessman and travel writer of unmitigated banality, he was entirely unqualified for the post which had been procured for him by a family friend. He had devised a model plan for workhouses for 500 residents based on a courtyard plan, with men and women separated by a 12ft-high wall down the middle. There was a single privy on each side of the building. Inmates were to be kept in small dormitories about 3.5 by 4.5m, each holding eight people in four double beds

By July 1835, Head had established eleven unions in East Kent, where the Swing Riots had started, and where an example had to be set. Two more were created in Sevenoaks and Penshurst. His design was used in several new workhouse buildings, including Bridge, Cranbrook, Dartford, Dover, East Ashford, Malling and Tonbridge, but in practice was soon found to be wanting as it had no provision for a chapel, sick-room or lying-in room, and there were not enough privies or fireplaces. Although Head imposed his design in Kent, it was never adopted elsewhere.

By the time Head left Kent in December 1835 he had established ten more unions and by 1841 nineteen of Kent's twenty-seven unions had new workhouses. Others were built at Sevenoaks, Gravesend, Tenterden, Canterbury and Chatham by 1855. Head believed that large unions with big boards could not be intimidated, and as befitted a model poor law county, the capacities of the new workhouses were large. The workhouse at Greenwich held over 1,000.

In terms of expenditure on the poor, the system worked. Outdoor relief was curtailed and never completely abolished, but Kent's poor law expenditure dropped from £345,878 in 1834 to £185,309 in 1837. It started to rise again later but never to the same level. The managers of the workhouses, elected Guardians, were ratepayers who had a vested interest in ensuring that workhouses were cheap to run.

One of the first new establishments to open for business was Thanet Union workhouse, built just north of the village of Minster, which opened its doors a week before Christmas 1835. With a quite startling lack of festive spirit, seven aged couples were moved there to be split up and fed on a basic diet of bread, oatmeal and meatless suet pudding. Conditions were primitive. There was no drainage system and water had to be hand drawn from the single well. Privies were emptied onto an open cesspit in the kitchen garden. Heating was minimal, and the inmates slept on straw paillasses covered by a coarse blanket.

The aged of Thanet were soon joined by orphans and single, pregnant women. The Guardians of the workhouse, in particularly vindictive mood, decreed that such women should wear a badge of shame, a gown with yellow sleeves, except on Sundays. Punishments were equally harsh. In 1848, three girls who complained about the suet pudding were confined on bread and water for a week. One of them was placed in 'the cage', an underground unlit cell, for twenty-four hours.

Thanet Union was not exceptional in the severity of its regime. At Milton Union workhouse, punishment often included confinement in 'The Black Hole', so named because it was, in fact, a coal hole where inmates, including children, were regularly shut up for twenty-four hours on a bread and water diet. In 1842, the master of Hoo workhouse was sent to prison for assaulting teenage girls. For very minor offences he would force them to strip and flog them until they bled. He said he was following orders, which technically he was, since his actions were permitted by the rule book. The scandal forced the Guardians to ban corporal punishment of women and girls.

Unsurprisingly, inmates attempted to escape. Boys were the most frequent culprits. In 1838, three boys confined in Tonbridge workhouse rose early, put

The Smack Boys' Home in the port of Ramsgate. It is now home to the harbour master and his staff.
(Anne Thompson)

their bolsters under their blankets to fool the authorities, and climbed out of the windows. Then they 'scampered for some hours over the countryside'. They were sentenced to three weeks in prison with hard labour. At Milton Union workhouse an iron grid was placed over the windows of the boys' dormitories to prevent escape and there were iron spikes on the exterior walls.

But there were examples of kindliness. In 1841, the Guardians of Faversham workhouse reprimanded the master for his harshness of manner, and instructed him to be kind but firm. Hollingbourne workhouse managed to maintain order without ever locking up a single inmate. Some workhouses supported or encouraged inmates to emigrate to the colonies, New Zealand and Canada being popular destinations. Holligbourne Union was particularly active in this respect, sending groups of forty or fifty abroad at a time. Some of these were orphaned children, sent to act as domestic or agricultural labourers. Despite charitable motives, in practice the scheme left the unaccompanied children open to exploitation and abuse.

Other children were put out as apprentices. Boys from Minster work-house, some as young as 10, were apprenticed to the fishing smack skippers at Ramsgate. When not at sea, however, they were left to their own devices, and, shocked by their plight, Canon Brenan, Vicar of Christ Church, Ramsgate, put pressure on the Board of Trade to provide them with accom-modation. The Smack Boys' Home was the result. No other British fishing port appears to have copied this unique facility.

Improvements in workhouse conditions came gradually. The children at Milton had swings to play on by the 1880s and were allowed toys in the 1890s. The Guardians started to allow charitable organisations to visit. At Thanet, meals of roast beef and plum pudding were served at Christmas and days of national rejoicing, paid for by Sir Moses Montefiore, a local benefactor.

The 1834 Act allowed for the education of the children living in the work-houses, and most medium to large establishments had their own schools. Reading and writing were taught, but the emphasis was on religion and the catechism. The quality of teaching was patchy. At Thanet, the first three masters were consecutively dismissed for using bad language, or beating the children without the master being present. The fourth was obliged to hand in his resignation after being found beating boys with stinging nettles to cure them of bed wetting. Milton Union workhouse also had a rapid turnover of teachers. The schoolmaster there was dismissed after he sexu-ally abused his pupils, and his wife was charged with teaching the children how to pilfer.

Elementary education outside the workhouse was also patchy and entirely unregulated. It was provided, for a fee, by individuals who decided that they were qualified to impart learning to the children of the middling sort. For those who could afford to send their offspring to school beyond elementary level, the existing grammar schools made provision, although they too had to adapt to changing times. Folkestone's Harvey School in 1819 rejected Latin in favour of navigation, which would be more useful to local boys. Sir Roger Manwood's School in Sandwich fell into decline and eventual abeyance in 1858 when only a few pupils remained. Its tempo-rary demise was blamed by the local people on its lack of utility: their sons had no need of the Latin and Greek which formed most of the curriculum. It was not re-opened until 1895.

The site of the Roger Manwood School in Sandwich from 1563 until the mid-nineteenth century. When it re-opened in 1895, it was in a new, modern building. (Anne Thompson)

There were, as well as the established grammar schools, an increasing number of often ephemeral academies and private boarding schools training young ladies in the social graces. In 1819, there were over 200 of these in East Kent alone, and by 1847 there were two dozen each at Ramsgate and Dover. Faversham had, in the course of the nineteenth century, nearly fifty girls' schools, most lasting less than five years. Typically, these offered tuition in a variety of accomplishments including drawing, music, shorthand and, in one case, 'fancy leather work'.

Private elementary schools were supplemented by charity schools for the poor, such as those at Ashford and Deal. Religious instruction was the mainstay of these establishments, followed by reading, writing (which was still taught separately and later) and basic arithmetic. Throughout the nineteenth century there were calls for free schooling for all children, which were blocked by politicians who feared that educating the working class would 'render them fractious and refractory'.

Religious differences also muddied the water. The non-conformist British and Foreign School Society was established in 1810 to provide schools for non-Anglican Protestant children. Alarmed, the next year the Church of England established The National Society for Promoting the Education of the Poor in the Principles of the Established Church throughout England and Wales (usually, for obvious reasons, abbreviated to The National Society), which set up Anglican church schools known as National Schools. By the middle of the nineteenth century there were eighteen British and Foreign schools in Kent, mostly in towns, including Maidstone, Chatham, Canterbury and Margate. The National Society aimed to have a school in every parish, but did not always succeed. An early Kent example was the National School in Faversham, built in 1814.

The elementary schools were supplemented by Sunday schools, which had the advantage that poor children could work and still receive an education. There were four in Faversham by 1843. Lamberhurst School started life in 1833 as a Sunday school, affiliated to the National Society. It had two rooms each 4m by 4.5m, one for boys and one for girls. Ten years later it was offering weekday classes as well and had extended to accommodate an attendance of sixty-five boys and forty-five girls.

For under-educated adults, night schools were being created. By 1849, fifteen mechanics' institutes and literary and scientific institutions had been founded for adults in Kent's main towns, from Deptford in the west to Margate in the east, attracting tradesmen anxious to improve themselves. The largest was at Greenwich with over 1,000 members, and the smallest at Bexley Heath with only fifty. Regardless of size, they nearly always had their own library attached, with from a hundred to over 8,000 volumes. The Faversham Literary and Scientific Institution was founded in 1846 and had its own museum. Displays included: the jaw of a swordfish, a chameleon, a parrot and a white rat (all stuffed) and a case of insects, also dead. Sometimes the education offered was more diverse. Lamberhurst, for example, had a 'Learned Society' which put on lectures on edifying subjects such as 'Modern Fortification', or 'The Polar Regions'.

The philanthropic ideal that all children should receive at least a basic education began to take hold. The government started to support both the non-conformist and Anglican societies through grants to build

The headmistresses' log book for Hythe National School in the 1870s notes laconically, 'Attendance much smaller on account of many of the children going hop-gathering.' (Author's collection)

schoolhouses, but the classrooms were not always full. Agriculture had a huge effect on the education of poor children. A Royal Commission on Education in 1869 reported that many children, especially in hop-growing districts, were employed by their parents at occasional work 'from infancy'. At Wateringbury, they were told there was a great demand for boys to work in the fields and that it was a 'serious inconvenience' for them to go to school. Girls were needed to stay at home for domestic work. At Wingham, the Commissioners found that the eldest girl was not sent to school so that she could look after younger children while her mother worked on the land. Elsewhere in Kent the Commissioners learned of children being involved up to seven months a year in such jobs as shaving hop-poles, bird-scaring, hay-making, pig-keeping, minding horses and sowing potatoes. Some parishes had set up night schools for these children, but they were rarely successful, as both children and teachers were too exhausted to attend regularly.

Things began to move forward, however, in 1869 when the National Education League began its campaign for free, compulsory and non-religious education for all children. The next year, an Education Act was quickly passed, the very first piece of legislation to deal specifically with the provision of education in England. Most importantly, it demonstrated a commitment to provision on a national scale.

The Act allowed voluntary schools to carry on unchanged, but established a system of school boards to build and manage schools in areas where they were needed. The boards were locally elected bodies which drew their funding from the local rates. Unlike the voluntary schools, religious teaching in the board schools was to be non-denominational.

The Act was not universally welcomed. The citizens of Canterbury called a public meeting to argue that board schools were completely unnecessary in the city. A letter-writer to the *Kentish Gazette* the following week summed up the people's opposition as being the expense to the rate payer. The Vicar of Maidstone told other Anglican clergymen in the area that they should oppose board schools and if this failed to ensure that they obtained a majority on the board so that Anglican values were taught in the new schools.

By 1880, nearly every Kent parish had a religious school or a board school. There were also experiments with industrial schools, to teach the poorest children, usually orphans, basic skills. The Kent County Industrial School for Girls aged 9 and above was opened in Greenwich in 1874 for up to thirty-six girls. Girls spent three hours a day on academic subjects and another six learning needlework, laundry and housework. The next year, an industrial school for boys was opened at Kingsnorth, near Ashford. The industrial element here consisted of handicrafts and gardening.

The girls' school was not a success. It was housed in a modified dwelling-house, with cramped accommodation, and in January 1876 three of the girls tried to set fire to the building by burning a mattress in their dormitory. The following year saw a small crimewave in the area, which was blamed on the school's residents. The culprits were sent to reformatories, but despite provision of better recreational facilities, problems persisted and the school was shut in 1884. The boys' school, in purpose-built premises with extensive grounds, was more successful, and endured, in one form or another, until the 1940s.

A new Education Act of 1880 made elementary education compulsory for all children from the ages of 5 to 10. Once again there was considerable opposition in agricultural areas which relied on child labour. Between March and October, children watched grazing animals and scared birds with clappers and rattles; in June they helped with shearing sheep, weeding cornfields and stone picking; in July it was pea-cutting, haymaking and cutting fruit for the London market; in September hopping, picking acorns for pig-food or blackberrying. In winter, boys could find good work as beaters at shooting parties at grand houses, and, later in the century, caddying at golf courses.

Local Attendance Committees were set up by magistrates to try to enforce attendance, but with mixed results. The headmistress of Ditton School said that it did not matter how often parents were warned by magistrates for keeping their children from school, it made no difference, but at Hartlip, attendance was far better.

Areas of Kent which concentrated on growing hops really struggled with school attendance. The nineteenth century was the golden age of the hop industry, with most of the national acreage in Kent. Early in the century David Colgate, a Chevening farmer, discovered a wild hop growing in a hedgerow, cultivated it and named it after himself. It proved a very hardy, very heavy cropper and reigned supreme in hop circles until Richard Fuggle of Brenchley bred the Fuggle hop in 1875.

Hops were a huge success story for the county; they could earn a farmer large sums of money, but their cultivation was labour intensive. Regular men were employed for much of the year, on such tasks as digging, dressing, creosoting and putting up poles. Women tied hops in May and June and made hop-pockets. Children 'shaved' hop poles to make them smooth, chopped up rags for manure and helped with the harvesting.

The hopping year started in October, immediately after the harvest. Then the old bines were carried away, poles removed and stacked and the ground heavily fertilised. Hops are perennials which grow from ground level and are trained up poles. In the early days, alder was used, but later chestnut was favoured. The poles had a limited life until creosote became available in about 1862. Various systems of wiring the hop bines to the poles were tried until finally Henry Burcher of Faversham worked out an economic wirework system which was widely copied. As the poles were high, up to 7m tall, the top wires were tied in by 'stringers' walking on stilts.

Much manpower was used on trying to combat the various pests to which hops are subject, although flea beetle and aphids were difficult to control before the development of modern pesticides. One remedy for the pernicious wireworm was to bury half a potato each day next to each plant to tempt wireworms away from the tender crops. Mould was another bugbear until it was discovered in about 1850 that dusting with sulphur helped control it.

Hops were ready for harvesting towards the end of August, according to variety, as the small, rough 'burs' changed into plump, yellow hops which had to be picked as soon as they were ripe. Picking required a huge workforce, far more than the local area could supply, even taking women and children into account.

The hop-picking season brought tremendous upheaval to otherwise quiet country villages. In the mid-nineteenth century the pickers, Irish, gypsies and Londoners, arrived a week or ten days before they were needed to ensure employment. They were generally regarded with suspicion, were believed to have 'filthy and disorderly habits' and to destroy fences and rob orchards. No one wanted to house them. A few growers built shed-like accommodation, but it was more usual to provide straw and hurdles and leave the pickers to build shelters with these. In the late 1860s, some still arrived on foot, despite the special hopper trains which then operated to bring pickers to stations on the line between Tunbridge Wells and Maidstone. Growers sent wagons to the stations to meet the trains.

The pickers worked in groups, often family-based, of eight to ten. Hops were picked into 'bins', canvas bags slung between 'X'-shaped supports. The 'bin-man' in charge of each group cut the hop bine close to its base, levered up the hop-pole on which it climbed with a tool called a hop-dog, and laid it lengthways across the 'V'-shaped bin ends for the hops to be stripped off. Children unable to reach the bins picked hops into an open umbrella. Payment was by the bushel and measurers came round at intervals to measure the hops into baskets holding eight or ten bushels. In Biddenden in 1855, pickers got a shilling per seven bushels.

Drying had to be done as soon as possible after picking, and this was carried out in an oast. The oast comprised an area where the hops were received, a drying floor above the kiln and a cooling room. Hop drying was a skilled and delicate art, as the hops needed to retain a little moisture. There were no mechanical instruments to measure moisture content, and only the dryer's nose, hands and experience could judge when they were ready.

Hops were brought in by horse and cart and spread evenly onto a 'hair', a horse hair mat which would smoulder but not catch fire on the slatted drying floor above the fierce heat of the kiln. Spread over half a metre deep, the hops were dried for about nine hours and turned with a broad canvas scupper. Sulphur was burned in large quantities during the drying process because it gave the hops a bright and uniform appearance.

After cooling, they were scuppered down into a huge canvas pocket suspended from the cooling floor, and pressed down until the pocket was crammed full. A 'bagster' was responsible for ensuring that every space in the pocket was filled by standing on top of the hops and treading them down.

An iconic round Kentish oast house. Many have now been converted into private dwellings.
(Anne Thompson)

The Hoppers' Hospital at Five Oak Green. The board over the door reads: *In happy memory of Old Friends who loved hopping and who loved this place very dearly who gave their lives for Old England and for us. 1914–1918. Lord all pitying Jesus Blest Grant them Thine Eternal Rest.* (Anne Thompson)

The archetypal Kent oast with its round kiln was not introduced until the beginning of the nineteenth century. The design was perfected by John Read from Horsmonden, a prolific inventor whose monument in Horsmonden church records that he also invented the stomach pump. They were only built for about a century. In around 1900, square oasts were found to work just as well and had the advantage of being cheaper to build.

Records show the same families visiting the same hop farms for generations, although until the twentieth century conditions could be dire. The Revd J.J. Kendon, visiting Goudhurst in the 1860s, said that hoppers slept 'like cattle in the field'. In response, he founded the Weald of Kent Hop-pickers Mission which, by 1889, had a team of over a dozen missionaries. Through the efforts of philanthropic and religious societies, decent accommodation began to be provided and in 1910 the Hoppers' Hospital was founded by an Augustinian priest, Father Richard Wilson, in Five Oak Green.

Conditions gradually improved, especially between the wars, by which time there were mission huts of many denominations in most of the larger hop gardens, and hot and cold running water and toilets. By the interwar years, the annual pilgrimage to the Kent hop fields had become a working holiday for many east London families. It was a source of extra cash, fresh air, a reunion with old friends, and a chance for some fun, much of which centred around the village pub. Mechanisation of picking in the 1960s meant the sad end of a long tradition.

Nine

STAYING ALIVE

I n the nineteenth century, communities began to be aware of how, working together, they could tackle public safety and public health issues and make improvements. Many Kent institutions and organisations that have become unremarkable facts of life had their origins in these years.

In all towns and villages, fire was a particular threat to life and property. The combination of wood-framed houses, thatched roofs and wood- or coal-burning fires was literally incendiary. The first advances in dealing with the problem came through private enterprise, not philanthropy. Fire insurance companies offered, in return for a premium, to attend with fire-fighting equipment if your house caught fire. The Kent Fire Office, established in 1802, was the first to operate in the county, and also rewarded people who helped extinguish fires on property insured by them.

In 1804, the company created its own fire brigade in Deptford, comprising twelve men. The men got a uniform, but no pay, as their reward was a certificate exempting them from impressment into the navy. In the same year, the company supplied two manual fire engines and enrolled men to handle them in Maidstone. Each man was provided with a rattle to raise the alarm. Early manual fire engines had two or four pumps operated by a long handle on each side, by which as many men as possible carried the engine to the fire, although later models were mounted on wheels. By 1821, engines had been supplied to nine other Kent towns and by 1850 Maidstone was protected by engines belonging to the Kent Fire Office, the Norwich Union and the Sun Fire Insurance Office.

The efforts of the fire insurance companies were replicated in towns where they did not operate by volunteer fire brigades. The first was established at Hythe in 1802, and another at Ashford not long afterwards and although slow to catch on, between 1840 to 1870 at least fourteen volunteer brigades were set up in Kent, including at Hawkhurst in 1843 and Cranbrook in 1844.

At Gravesend that year, a combined effort was needed to tackle a huge fire which broke out in a shrimp-boiling house in West Street, an area full of the wooden dwelling houses of the poor and warehouses stuffed with flammable goods. Fire engines from Gravesend, Dartford, Rochester and Crayford attended, but the wind was fresh and the fire spread. People living in adjoining streets were evacuated and houses demolished, but the flames blew towards Union Wharf, where pitch, tar and timber were stored. Having destroyed the wharf, the fire spread to a depot holding barrels of gunpowder and sulphur. Two of the barrels were rolled into the Thames before the warehouse caught light, but the rest exploded and the blast flattened nearby houses. The fire was not extinguished until the next morning when the wind subsided. The town started a fund for re-housing the now homeless poor, but two years later West Street was again the source of a fierce blaze which destroyed twenty-five of the newly built houses.

Often it took a disastrous fire before a fire brigade was formed. Chatham brigade was formed in 1866, after a fire had burned for seven days at a wharf, and the same year Whitstable started its own brigade after a fire destroyed both public and dwelling houses. However, it was not able to deal effectively with the next conflagration to hit the town in 1869. This was not unusual. Sandgate fire brigade was formed 1859, but by 1877 they had lost most of their buckets which had apparently been 'borrowed' for pigswill, and when a fire broke out that year, no one could find the key to the engine house. When they found it, they could not get the engine out. When they finally got it to the fire, the engine turned out to be useless. Even so, it was another five years before an appeal was started to buy a modern fire-engine.

The rescue of people trapped in fire remained rudimentary, relying on builders' ladders and ropes until, in 1836, the Royal Society for the Protection of Life from Fire was formed. It provided wheeled escapes which could be extended up to 18m and had canvas troughs down which trapped people could slide to the ground. Kent fire brigades began to acquire them.

Deal fire brigade, formed in 1874, bought one of the escapes, and took it around the town, presumably with an educational intent. Instead, it turned into something of an attraction, and the town's citizens had great fun throwing themselves out of high buildings onto the canvas trough. However, since the brigade did not actually own a fire engine, it attracted censure from the local press, which called the escape 'an expensive toy'. A fire engine was duly bought the next year.

The fire brigade at Lydd was one of the last to be formed, in 1890. The town council bought a building to use as a fire station, and sensibly

A fire brigade display in Hythe in 1905. The engine is pumping water from the Royal Military Canal. (Author's collection)

removed its thatch. They bought a fine Merryweather fire engine, although it was still hand-pumped. To try it out and provide a little local show, the brigade carried the hose up the steeple of Lydd church and was then able to throw a jet of water from the nozzle another 19m in the air. Public display and competitions were an important part of the routine of early fire brigades. Competitions were run by the National Fire Brigades Union, with individual and team events in fire drill. Lydd brigade won the National Manual Challenge Cup in 1903, and the team was welcomed home with flags, bunting and cheering crowds.

A good supply of water was necessary for effective fire-fighting. In villages, the brigades sometimes pumped the village pond dry in their efforts, but in towns they relied on existing water supply systems. By the early eighteenth century, most Kent towns had some provision. Water was drawn from rivers and springs and supplied to the public through tanks, pumps, wells and conduits, or sometimes delivered by water-carts.

Water was crucial to the health of the county. Contaminated drinking water could, and during the nineteenth century often did, lead to outbreaks of cholera. Between 1831 and 1866 there were a series of epidemics. The disease killed quickly, and created panic, especially as its early symptoms could be confused with the dysentery which affected many every summer. The difference was that by the next day the cholera victim would be dead. There was no cure.

The outbreaks highlighted the need for clean water and adequate sewerage. Observations made in Tonbridge during the 1854 outbreak recorded cottages with privies within a metre of the back door. When emptied, their contents could sometimes be left lying on the ground for days before collection. Elsewhere in the town, privies drained directly into a stream which fed the water supply. The same year cholera killed forty-eight at Sandgate. This was a town which had only recently, at considerable expense, made huge improvements to its drainage and water supply, but investigations showed the new drains to be blocked and leaking. The old cesspools had not been properly sealed off and water supplies were still polluted. Cholera outbreaks in the villages on the Medway were said to be caused by the presence of seasonal hop-pickers, whose faeces ended up in streams which drained into the water supply, because farm owners would not provide them with proper facilities.

Hop pickers were blamed, often unfairly, for all manner of social ills. (Author's collection)

Human waste in drinking water also caused typhoid, another Victorian killer. The largest ever reported epidemic in the United Kingdom was an outbreak in Maidstone in 1897. Facilities were overwhelmed and there were national collections of food and medicines for the town. Nurses, among them a young Edith Cavell, were brought from London to deal with over 1,800 patients, of whom 132 died. Pollution from a spring which fed the East Farleigh Waterworks was blamed, and hop pickers identified as the carriers of the disease. They were perhaps a convenient scapegoat and distracted attention from the fact that the town had a poor drainage system, with many domestic privies badly connected to the sewage system.

Freedom from infected water marked the end of the great epidemics but the cost of new water supplies and proper drainage was considerable, and there was nearly always opposition from ratepayers. In some places, progress was very slow indeed: Gravesend still lacked a proper water supply as late as 1909.

When the well-off were sick, whether with cholera, typhoid or any other disease, they paid for a doctor's attendance, medicine and nursing care. When the poor were sick, there was little provision, although those in the north of the county might be sent to the free London hospitals. Dartford's patients were sent to St Thomas's or Guy's, those from Farningham to St Bartholomew's. The Kent and Canterbury Hospital, opened in April 1793, was the first general hospital for the Kent poor. Its rules were clear that no one who could afford to pay for treatment was to be admitted, and its acceptance criteria were limited. It did not accept anyone with a contagious or venereal disease, or consumption, anyone who was plainly incurable or those who were 'not clean in person or apparel'. Financed originally by a legacy, it remained dependant on donations and subscribers. Some parishes outside Canterbury became subscribers and could then send their poor to the city for treatment.

In spring 1796, a Quaker physician, John Lettsom, opened the Royal Sea Bathing Hospital in Margate, the first orthopaedic hospital in the world. The *Gentleman's Magazine* reported that 'the building is constructed in a very commodious manner ... near the beach ... and a bathing machine was built for the sole use of the patients'. Each poor patient, recommended by a subscribing governor, had first to be examined by a medical board in

Barming Asylum, or the Kent County Lunatic Asylum. The barred windows can clearly be seen. (Author's collection)

London, and was then ferried down to Margate by hoy, one of the single-masted sloops which plied the London to Kent route. Most of them were suffering from tuberculosis of the bones or joints. Over the course of the nineteenth century the hospital expanded considerably, funded by rich benefactors, Queen Victoria included.

Many towns started to provide dispensaries which distributed free medicine and advice to the poor. Ramsgate and St Lawrence Dispensary was opened in 1820 and Tunbridge Wells started its Dispensary for Poor People in 1829. The Canterbury Dispensary used 8,712 leeches in 1830, and had a drugs bill of over £300 in 1850. The dispensaries were supported by subscription and local doctors. In recognition of the need for nursing care and surgery, they began to take in-patients. The West Kent Hospital in Maidstone, opened in 1832, had its origins in this way, as did Folkestone Hospital twelve years later and Dover Hospital in 1851.

There began to be some provision for mental health patients, too, although in its earliest stages containment rather than care was the priority. The Kent County Lunatic Asylum for '160 pauper inmates and 50 dangerous idiots' was built 3km outside Maidstone on Barming Heath and opened in 1833. In common with other psychiatric hospitals of the time, it was modelled on a prison – indeed, it was designed by the same architect that built Maidstone Prison. It had massive stone walls, small barred windows, and a lack of any home comforts. Inmates were often restrained. A report of 1841 tells of two men chained to their beds for over four years, but by 1844 the authorities were starting to look at the place as somewhere a cure might be effected. In the next two decades, improvements were made, with games allowed and proper mattresses provided for beds instead of straw paillasses. Although progress continued to be made, with an inmates' orchestra, pictures on the walls, potted plants, and magic lantern shows, the nursing care was rudimentary and focused on prevention of escapes. Restraints were used less, but patients were often controlled by the use of hypnotic drugs. It was not until the twentieth century that trained psychiatric nurses were employed.

Nearly forty years after the opening of Barming Asylum, another facility was needed, and St Augustine's Hospital was built as the East Kent Asylum in 1872. It clearly illustrated a change in attitude. The site chosen, on Chartham Downs, satisfied the more enlightened requirements of the Commissioners in Lunacy: a site on elevated ground with cheerful prospects and enough space to provide employment and recreation for inmates while preventing them being overlooked or disturbed by strangers. Originally built to house 870 patients, the hospital gradually expanded and became a self-contained village, with its own farm, workshops, baker, butcher, fire-brigade, church, graveyard, gasworks, cricket team and band.

Meanwhile, some of the City of London's psychiatric patients were being housed at the new asylum at Stone, near Dartford, as the city authorities were unable to find either a local property to act as an asylum or a big enough space in which to build one. The buildings were designed in a mock Tudor style, on a hilltop with panoramic view to the Thames, and were completed in 1866.

Alongside fire brigades and hospitals, the third emergency service, the police force, was also being developed. Before the nineteenth century, law enforcement in Kent, as in the rest of England, was provided by town constables, unpaid and sometimes reluctant 'volunteers' drawn from the local population. The constable's duties were confined to his parish and he did not concern himself with matters elsewhere: even had he been interested he would in all probability have been unable to read any communications. *In extremis*, magistrates could call the military in, as happened at the Battle of Bossenden Wood.

In 1822, Home Secretary Sir Robert Peel told Parliament that the country should have 'a vigorous system of police'. The Metropolitan Police Force was formed in 1829, but it was not until 1835 that an Act of Parliament required all boroughs to set up a police force. The response in Kent was unenthusiastic, and two years later only just over half of Kent towns had taken action. In some places, such as Sandwich and Tenderden, the 'force' was a solitary constable.

Canterbury was one of the earliest to set up a police force. In February 1836, the city appointed a superintendent, two inspectors and fifteen constables to patrol the streets in a uniform based on that worn by the Metropolitan Police – a navy swallow-tailed coat and navy trousers topped off with a stovepipe hat. Most of the Canterbury constables were labourers, while others were local tradesmen. Inevitably, there was some opposition, as the force was funded through the rates and angry letters were written to the local press demanding fewer policemen. Perhaps indicative of its standing in the city, the new force was housed in a disused abattoir, then later in part of the workhouse. There was a high turnover of constables, and a number of dismissals for misconduct, usually for the offences of being either drunk or asleep on duty.

Drunkenness bedevilled borough police forces. Five Deal officers were disciplined for accepting beer from one of their own prisoners; at both Gravesend and Dover the inspectors were dismissed for being under the influence; a Folkestone constable was dismissed for drinking rum in The Fountain public house while on duty. Other offences included buying food for non-existent prisoners, being absent from a beat, bad and insulting language, refusing to go on duty, being violent, allowing prisoners to escape, consorting with a prostitute, and fraud.

Folkestone Town Hall was opened in 1861. The authorities managed to combine an expression of civic pride with the necessity of providing a police station, which they hid away in the basement. (Anne Thompson)

In 1856, the government acted to achieve some conformity in the forces, and passed an Act to introduce county forces, led by a chief constable. The next year the Kent County Constabulary was born. On 19 May 1857, 222 constables were sworn in and were drilled at Maidstone barracks. Strict conditions as to their physical attributes and background had been laid down. Ten days later they left to take up their duties. The need for proper police stations became pressing. Lock-ups had usually been provided by boroughs, and where there was only one constable, his own house was the point of contact for the public. A flurry of building ensued, starting in 1864 at Chatham and ending in 1868 in Sandwich.

The new county constabulary was surprisingly mobile. In 1870, two Ashford officers sailed to Brisbane to arrest their own superintendent, who had fled there with a lady friend after stealing £350 from a prisoner. Investigations showed this to be just the last in a series of abuses of his position in which he was aided by the silence of his colleagues. He was returned to England and sentenced to seven years' penal servitude.

The new force's first loss in the line of duty was Constable Israel May, stationed at Snodland, who in 1873 was attacked and killed with his own truncheon. Near the scene were found items belonging to one Thomas Atkins who, when arrested, said he had acted in self-defence. He was con-victed of manslaughter.

For some years the county force existed alongside the old borough forces. The work of these local officers was very much to do with nuisances – hawkers, unruly children, stray and rabid dogs, lost property, drunken-ness – or small-scale and rural crimes – illegal gaming, pick-pocketing, burglary, poaching and, especially on the Romney Marsh, sheep-stealing.

At Chatham Naval Dockyard, a separate Dockyard Police Force was established in 1835 to deal with on-site crime, which consisted mostly of theft from the stores. It was not, apparently, particularly effective, and a review carried out at the Admiralty's request by the Metropolitan Police concluded that it was ill-trained and too many of the men had local connections, with all that implied. In 1860, the Metropolitan Police took over policing the dockyard, and remained there until 1932. Oddly, to modern understanding of police work, they dealt not only with crime, but with apprentices who absented themselves from work without good reason. Offenders were punished by being locked in the cells for a few hours.

In 1888, by Act of Parliament, the small borough forces were amalgamated with the county constabularies and the beginnings of a recognisably modern police force began to emerge. All Kent police applicants had to undergo a medical to ensure their ability to serve. Physical fitness was encouraged and annual sports days and cricket tournaments were established. Police housing was provided for both married and single men. Although there was no professional training beyond drilling, voluntary classes in police law and procedure were offered from 1903. A Detective Branch was founded and in 1904 every division was issued with a fingerprint outfit. From 1911, photographs were taken of prisoners.

The men and women the police arrested were likely to end up in prison, which also changed significantly through the nineteenth century. Eighteenth- and early nineteenth-century prisons in Kent, as elsewhere, were of various sorts. The boroughs had their own prisons, often no more than lock-ups for vagrants and drunks, or for those awaiting trial. Some towns had Houses of Correction where short sentences could be served. There were also two county prisons, in Maidstone and Canterbury, for those serving longer sentences, and debtors' prisons. They were all invariably squalid, filthy places, which started to attract the attention of philanthropic campaigners. When the Quaker prison reformer John Howard visited Maidstone Prison in 1776 he commented on the smallness of its courtyards and the lack of air and light. He correctly predicted an outbreak of gaol fever, a louse-borne illness arising from overcrowding, and in 1783 twenty-two prisoners and a craftsman working at the prison were killed by the disease. The authorities acted, and when Howard next visited he was pleased to see some improvements had been made, including provision of an infirmary.

The gaol was rebuilt between 1811 and 1819, at a cost of nearly £2,000 and to correspondingly loud howls of dismay from ratepayers. It could house 450 felons. A spinning manufactory was set up to keep them usefully occupied, but in 1824 a treadmill was introduced for grinding corn and raising water. Both men and women worked on this, six hours a day, climbing the equivalent of 2,633m. Punishment for infringing prison regulations was whipping or confinement in a dark cell. The diet was inadequate.

Maidstone Prison is one of the oldest penal institutions in the United Kingdom, having been in operation for over 200 years. The original perimeter wall still stands. (Anne Thompson)

Major Bannister, the Maidstone Prison governor, had difficulty in preventing inmates from collecting and eating raw potatoes, potato peelings and dirty roots, while a prison inspector reported 'the marks of starvation on some prisoners' faces in the wheel sheds'.

As with attitudes to the poor, popular and official opinion about the treatment of prisoners hardened as the nineteenth century drew on, and in 1865 the treadmill became a compulsory element of a custodial sentence. At the county prison at Canterbury, built in 1806, men worked the open-air mills nine hours a day. The prison's surgeon complained that their diet was insufficient to maintain this level of exercise. At Dover Gaol, which had no treadmill, prisoners were set to handcranking machines. These were iron drums on legs with a handle on one side and a dial which recorded the number of turns made. Male convicts had to complete 14,000 revolutions a day and failure resulted in punishment or the withholding of food. This unproductive and soul-destroying activity was carried out in solitary confinement. Both handcranks and treadwheels were finally made illegal in 1899, by which time all prisons had been taken out of the control of local authorities and were run by central government.

The other penal establishments in Kent were the prison hulks, vessels no longer needed for active service which were moored on the Medway and at Woolwich. They were first used on a large scale to house French prisoners of war during the Napoleonic Wars, and later as floating prisons for felons, many awaiting transportation.

Life on board was grim and punishments were harsh. The hulks were overcrowded and disease-ridden. The *Brunswick* at Chatham crammed 460 prisoners in hammocks into a space 3.8m by 12m. Ventilation was limited to fourteen portholes, 43cm square. Cholera, typhus and smallpox were rife. During the day, the men laboured on the Chatham Dockyard improvements. Small wonder that Magwitch, in Dickens's *Great Expectations*, made such a desperate attempt at escape.

By 1847, the Medway hulks were no longer in use and those at Woolwich provided a convict convalescence service of sorts. A government inspector found that patients were verminous, bedding was rarely washed, toilets were inadequate and there were no green vegetables in the diet. The hulks were finally abandoned in 1857.

Not every convicted prisoner received a custodial sentence or was transported. Many were hanged. Kent's designated place of execution was on Penenden Heath, which necessitated a procession from Maidstone Gaol, where all convicts under sentence of death were held, to the gallows, a distance of over 3km. Occasionally, up until the eighteenth century, felons were returned to the scene of their crime and hung in chains there, their bodies left swinging to rot or be eaten by the crows, as a warning to others. This was the fate of John Ogleby, a murderer, who in 1750 was executed at Oldberry Hill, near Sevenoaks.

Executions were public, and people living near Penenden Heath grew tired of the behaviour of the (often drunken) mob on execution days, when they trampled hedges and crops. The last public execution on the heath took place in 1830 when John Dyke was hanged for burning a hayrick, although it later emerged he was innocent. After that, hangings took place outside Maidstone Gaol, and, after 1868, in private inside it.

The last emergency service to emerge in Kent was help for shipping. The sea was a killer and with its long coastline and many hazards for sailors, Kent saw more than its fair share of wrecks. One of the most treacherous of these hazards was the Goodwin Sands. Situated 6.5km off Deal, 16km-long in part, and over 7km at their widest, they were so well known as a danger to shipping that Shakespeare mentioned them in *The Merchant of Venice*. Although hazardous, they serve as a breakwater and create between them and the coast a useful deep-water anchorage, the Downs. It was not until 1795 that the Goodwins were marked by a lightship, on their western edge, and later in the nineteenth century the eastern and southern edges were also marked. Attempts to erect a permanent beacon on the sands all proved futile, usually succumbing to bad weather or being run down by shipping.

In 1898, the radio transmission pioneer Marconi installed wireless equipment at the South Foreland lighthouse at St Margaret's Bay, near Dover, and established communication with the East Goodwin Lightship, anchored 19km away. The first ever use of wireless telegraphy as an aid to

The South Foreland lighthouse shone out over the Straits of Dover until 1988 when modern navigational aids made it redundant and it was decommissioned. In June 2012, it was relit in honour of the Diamond Jubilee of Queen Elizabeth II. (Author's collection)

ships in distress occurred on 11 March 1899 when the sailing ship *Elbe* ran onto the Goodwin Sands. The lightship communicated with the lighthouse; the lighthouse staff contacted the Ramsgate lifeboat station; the lifeboat attended and saved the stricken vessel. Marconi then obtained permission from the French Government to set up a wireless station in Wimereux, near Boulogne, and on 27 March 1899 Marconi himself sent the first ever wireless message between France and Britain to the South Foreland lighthouse. In 1909, the inventor established a wireless experimental station next to the North Foreland lighthouse to issue fog warnings to shipping.

As well as the Goodwins, there were innumerable other hazards round the Kent coast – the Longnose Ridge, Knock John, the Long Sand, the Wedge Sand, and the Tongue Sands among them. Despite the lighthouses and lightships, wrecks and loss of life were frequent. Local men usually did what they could to help, but until 1824, there was no collaborative system to provide assistance. In 1703, during the 'Great Storm', a cyclone which wreaked havoc in southern England, four naval ships were lost on the Goodwin Sands. The *Northumberland*, the *Mary*, the *Restoration* and the *Stirling Castle* all sank, with the loss of over 1,000 lives. According to Daniel Defoe, one Deal shopkeeper offered a reward to any man saving the life of sailors trapped on a sandbar, and thus was responsible for saving over 200 lives.

The National Institution for the Preservation of Life from Shipwreck, later the Royal National Lifeboat Institution (RNLI), was founded in 1824 by a number of dignitaries, including the Archbishop of Canterbury and William Wilberforce, concerned at the ad hoc nature of live-saving activities. One man who must have been pleased by this development was Lionel Lukin, the inventor of the first 'unimmergible boat'. He had sent a prototype of his brainchild, the *Experiment*, down to Ramsgate in 1795 to be tested. It was an unqualified success, even enabling its skipper to carry on his smuggling trade in the worst weather, an outcome not, presumably, intended by Lukin. However, his invention was adopted elsewhere and he lived to see the foundation of the RNLI before his death in Hythe, where he is laid to rest.

The RNLI raised funds to provide lifeboats and equipment to sea ports, and promoted the importance of life-saving equipment. Margate and

The grave of Lionel Lukin in Hythe. The extraordinarily long inscription engraved on both sides of his tombstone reads in part: *This Lionel Lukin was the first who built a life boat and was the original inventor of that principle of safety by which many lives and much property have been preserved from shipwreck.* (Anne Thompson)

Broadstairs were early beneficiaries. Margate bought its own lifeboat in 1850 and was given a second by a member of the Coutts banking family. News of the loss of the Irish packet *Royal Adelaide* with 250 lives, on the sands off Margate in 1850, may have been the prompt that led shipbuilder Thomas White to present one of his lifeboats to his home town of Broadstairs that summer. The lifeboat saw its first use on 6 March 1851, when the brig *Mary White* became trapped on the Goodwin Sands during a severe northerly gale. A ballad was written to celebrate the successful mission.

The RNLI took over the Broadstairs lifeboat station in 1868 and other stations followed, at Dover, Folkestone, Hythe, Dungeness and Littlestone, on the edge of the Romney Marsh. In 1856, the RNLI made an appeal for cash to establish a lifeboat station at Walmer. A site for a wooden boathouse was provided by a local man and a lifeboat acquired, a ten-oared self-righting vessel, the *Royal Thames Yacht Club*, so called because the funds to build it had all been raised by members of that institution. She was first launched on service on 5 January 1857, to rescue thirteen crew and two local boatmen from the barque *Reliance* that had been wrecked in rough seas and a severe gale, along with heavy snow, off Walmer. The wooden boathouse was eventually replaced with a stone building in a neo-Gothic style with a bell turret to summon the lifeboatmen.

The neo-Gothic architectural style of Walmer Lifeboat Station mirrors the design of St Saviour's church, which stands directly opposite it. (Anne Thompson)

Lifesaving efforts were not always successful. On 1 January 1860, the brig *Guttenburg* met with hurricane-force winds and heavy snow off the Goodwin Sands, where it capsized. Distress signals were fired but were not seen at Ramsgate harbour because of the weather. They were, however, spotted at Deal, and a lifeboatman there sent a telegram to Ramsgate asking for the assistance. The lifeboat *Northumberland* prepared to make a rescue attempt, but was prevented from leaving by the harbour master, because he had not received the distress call by the proper means, and regulations had not been observed. The delay resulted in the deaths of twenty-six passengers and crew. The harbour master was later charged with neglect, but retained his post

The failure to respond immediately to another ship in trouble, in similar blizzard conditions in 1875, became a national scandal. In December 1875, the German passenger ship *Deutschland*, bound for New York, lost her bearings and ran aground on the Kentish Knock, 5km off Margate. It took thirty hours for her distress flares to be seen and for help to arrive, and 168 were lost. Soon after the news of the disaster had broken, the wreck was raided by men from the nearby coastal towns, particularly Harwich and Ramsgate. The *Illustrated London News* published a drawing of the scene which depicted the wreckers as vultures and *The Times* reported that corpses had been ransacked and jewellery stolen.

Far more typical of the reputation of Kent lifesavers, though, was the honourable record of the Hythe lifeboatmen who, despite losing a crew member, persisted in their attempts to save the crew of *Benvenue*, which had struck bottom off Seabrook in 1891. All night and all the next day, in mountainous seas they struggled to reach the ship, finally succeeding in saving all but the captain and his wife. The coxswain and his assistant were awarded RNLI silver medals for their courage and endurance.

Ten

SUNDAYS, HIGH DAYS AND HOLIDAYS

Until the nineteenth century, the idea of 'leisure' was immaterial to most ordinary people whose days were filled with the labour necessary to stay alive. From the 1840s, legal restrictions on working hours began to take effect, and from 1871, workers benefitted from six bank holidays a year. Some were even lucky enough to get additional paid holidays, but this was rare until after the First World War. Sundays were, however, for most people, a day of rest.

Church-going was one way in which people might choose to spend their Sunday leisure hours, although the extent of Victorian piety is sometimes exaggerated. In 1851 only 50 per cent of Kent adults went to church on Sunday. Kent was not particularly irreligious – this was about the same proportion as the rest of the country. The highest attendance was in Maidstone, with 61 per cent.

Of those who did go to church in Kent, about half attended non-conformist places of worship. In 1689, after centuries of persecution and burnings, Parliament had passed the Act of Toleration, giving non-conformists liberty to worship God as they wished, though not, until 1828, to hold public or military office as well. Catholics got the same rights a year later, but Jews had to wait as late as 1890 for full emancipation.

Towns might have several non-conformist congregations, but in the early days they met at each other's houses rather than in a dedicated building. The new law required them to register these places as designated Meeting Houses. The Baptists of the village of Eythorne, for example, went to the Quarter Sessions at Canterbury in 1756, paid sixpence and registered a newly built hall owned by a local shoemaker as their legal meeting place.

Eythorne Baptist Church, still thriving today. (Anne Thompson)

Non-Anglican preachers also had to be licensed by the Sessions, too, and the Eythorne Baptists nominated thirteen men as well as their two ministers as 'duly qualified'. Their congregation grew, and the meeting house, which could seat sixty people, was doubled in size in 1773. At about the same time, another Baptist meeting house was built in Sandwich next to a stream which was diverted through it to provide a baptistery, where people from surrounding villages, such as Eythorne, could be baptised by immersion.

The Eythorne congregation continued to flourish, and in 1804 the church members were called together by a wealthy landowner, Peter Fector, who lived near their meeting house. He said he could no longer bear the sound of their enthusiastic singing, and offered to buy the place from them for £500 and to donate half a hectare of land out of earshot of his house. The new chapel was built that year.

The growing popularity of the sect is apparent in the size and scale of Dover Baptist Church, which was opened in 1840 in the town centre.

It could seat 400–500, held three services on Sundays and had week-night lectures and prayer meetings. Baptists were, however, most numerous in the Weald of Kent, where they constituted nearly 75 per cent of the church-going population. At Spillshill, near Staplehurst, a large congregation met even before the Act of Toleration. It splintered during the eighteenth century into factions: General Baptists and Particular Baptists. The General Baptists developed strong links with co-religionists in the USA, and many local families emigrated there in the 1840s and '50s.

A rival attraction for the non-conformist soul was Methodism, which started as an evangelical movement in the Church of England, but began to split away even before the death of its founder, John Wesley, in 1791. Methodist chapels were organised into circuits, with a superintendent minister. There was a circuit for Kent by 1766, and chapels in Canterbury and Chatham. Methodism, too, formed splinter groups. Only three were active in Kent: Wesleyans, Primitive Methodists and Bible Christians, although a group called Lady Huntingdon's Connection flourished briefly in Maidstone. The Wesleyan Methodists at Canterbury built themselves a handsome new chapel in 1811 which is still in use today.

An apostate from Methodism was William Booth, who founded the Salvation Army in 1878. Four years later, a branch opened in Maidstone. Like all early Salvationists, they faced opposition and even violence. That first year of their existence, there were riots when they attempted to march through town. The same happened in Wouldham, on the Medway, in 1890. Two youths charged with attacking them were brought to court but the magistrate remarked that the Salvationists 'brought trouble down on themselves'.

Bromley Salvationists had to contend with the 'Skeleton Army', prevalent throughout the South of England, who with their skull-and-crossbones banners violently disrupted Salvationists' marches and open-air meetings. In 1888, the disturbance they caused was so great that it took fifty policemen to restore order. The Skeletons taunted the Salvationists with slogans like 'Blood and Thunder', mocking the Salvation Army's war cry 'Blood and Fire'; or the 'three B's: Beef, Beer and Bacca', parodying the Army's three S's – 'Soup, Soap and Salvation'.

They provoked riots in Folkestone, too. Wright Griggs, a Hythe Salvationist, had helped defend the church premises against them, and in

1883 planned to marry his sweetheart in the same place. He heard that the Skeleton Army planned to bombard them with fish heads and offal, so the couple secretly went to Hythe and were safely married in the much less controversial Congregational church there.

Catholicism was weak in Kent, but even more unpopular than the Salvation Army, and the Catholic Emancipation Act in 1829 provoked a gathering of 30,000 outraged Protestants at Penenden Heath near Maidstone. Catholic church building was slow to take off, and often the first priest in a town was sent to minister to Irish Catholic soldiers garrisoned there, as at Chatham and Dover.

One early example of a permanent church was St Augustine's in Tunbridge Wells, built by Jesuit missionaries, apparently without opposition, but in Maidstone in 1851 when Henry Wilberforce, the Catholic convert son of the anti-slavery campaigner, tried to build a church, there was a public outcry. The authorities, bowing to public opinion, refused his application. Biding his time, Wilberforce brought an Italian priest into the town seven years later to celebrate mass at his home, and to offer instruction to Catholic children at the barracks. Finally, a proper church building was started in 1871 and opened in 1880.

St Paul's Roman Catholic church in Dover, funded by a bequest from a Catholic noblewoman, the Countess de Front, was opened in 1868. (Anne Thompson)

In 1850, the English Catholic hierarchy was restored, and the first Bishop of Southwark invited Benedictine monks to Ramsgate, where the architect Augustus Welby Pugin had built a Catholic church at his own expense. Augustus's son Edward Pugin designed the Catholic church of St Paul's in Dover.

There were even fewer Jews than Catholics in the county. In 1192, when Richard I was ransomed, it was the Canterbury Jews who were charged with collecting the ransom, but they, and all other Jews, were later expelled from England by Edward I in 1290. They started to drift back after Oliver Cromwell rescinded the expulsion order in 1656.

In 1762, a synagogue was built in St Dunstan's Street in Canterbury, but with the coming of the railway the land it stood on was compulsorily purchased, as it was the site of a planned level crossing. Money was raised for a new synagogue, which was built in King's Street with Sir Moses

The old synagogue in Canterbury, one of only a few surviving in the world built in the Egyptian revival style. (Anne Thompson)

Montefiore, a financier and philanthropist, laying the foundation stone in 1848. It included a Mikvah, a ritual bathhouse, in the grounds. It closed in the 1920s when the Jewish population had again declined.

Montefiore, who had a country estate in Thanet, had earlier founded the Ramsgate synagogue to commemorate his first visit to Jerusalem. It was consecrated on 17 June 1832, and although the Jewish population remained small, the town attracted Jewish visitors. In 1901, there were six kosher restaurants and boarding houses.

The Chatham Memorial Synagogue was the last in Kent to open in the nineteenth century and was built in 1869 by Simon Magnus in memory of his son Lazarus, on the site of an even older synagogue. Lazarus had been a successful businessman and served three terms as Mayor of Queenborough but died of an accidental overdose of chloroform at 39. In its cemetery, an ornate memorial records the achievements of Daniel Bamard, who owned theatres and music halls in Chatham, Dartford and London and who founded Chatham Fire Brigade.

All the churches and chapels offered worthy and improving activities to keep people away from the pubs and other unchristian activities – and from rival churches. In Maidstone, the Church of England set up the Anglican Church Institute, which had both literary and debating societies, while the Methodists there had a literary society for 'mutual improvement'.

For children, the Band of Hope aimed to encourage them to be abstainers from alcohol in adult life through education and through proving what fun could be had without strong drink. The only entry requirement was to 'sign the pledge' to forswear alcohol forever. Although it started out as an Anglican movement, it spread across denominations. In Sittingbourne in 1908, the Anglican, Methodist, Baptist and Congregational churches all had separate meetings. The group lasted well into the twentieth century, a Woodchurch headmistress recording a Band of Hope outing to Dymchurch in 1923.

The evils of excessive drinking among the working classes occupied the Victorians a great deal. The adult Temperance Movement did not prosper in Kent as well as it did in its heartlands in the North of England, but still had a presence in most towns. 'Temperance' could mean anything from advocacy of prohibition, to total abstinence to toleration of moderate drinking.

The movement had many, some short-lived, manifestations. In Deal, there were two teetotal temperance groups, both American in origin. The Independent Order of Good Templars flourished for a few years from 1872, and in 1882 the Blue Ribbon Gospel Movement was established. On I July of that year, it attracted 5,000 people to Walmer Castle for a temperance rally.

The Church of England Temperance Society was a more tolerant organisation, and did not insist on total abstinence, although many of its members were teetotal. It provided court missionaries, who would attend magistrate courts to help men and women brought before the bench for drunkenness. In 1913, there were nine such missionaries in Kent who worked in thirty-three different courts and were reported to have helped nearly 10,000 cases.

Most drinking, whether problematic or not, was done in public houses and most towns had a good selection. In 1829, Deal had thirty-nine public houses, although the town at this time was economically depressed and had a population of only about 7,000. There were also thirty-odd beer houses, which were not licensed to sell spirits and had shorter opening hours.

Kent brewers and public houses benefited enormously from the number of military personnel based in the county and some catered especially for them. The Fountain in Folkestone offered 'penny hangs' to drunk soldiers. Ropes were suspended across the ceiling, over which men who were too inebriated to make their way back to their barracks could drape themselves and fall into a drunken sleep. In the morning, the landlord would simply untie one end of the ropes.

One of the concerns of the Temperance Movement was the violence which alcohol could lead to, and they were not short of examples. In 1856 in Deal, Samuel Baker, the landlord of The Ship, drunkenly bludgeoned 19-year-old Lieutenant McCarroll to death because the younger man had insulted his wife. In 1905, Percy Murray, a potman at The Fountain in Deal, stabbed the landlord, Robert Pearce, to death because the latter had accused him of spying on his wife through a hole in her bedroom wall. The Radnor Inn in Folkestone was the scene of a riot by drunken railway labourers in 1843. They barricaded themselves inside and proceeded to attempt to drink the pub dry. The Riot Act was read, and the captain of

the coastguard, accompanied by forty men armed with cutlasses, muskets and pistols, arrived, whereupon the rioters sensibly gave themselves up peacefully.

A ready supply of hops ensured that there were plenty of breweries in Kent and many towns had their own which supplied local hostelries. Three among them became pre-eminent during the nineteenth century.

Shepherd Neame claims the title of Britain's oldest brewer, and has been making beer in Faversham since 1698. Its boast is that it still uses traditional methods. Every beer is brewed with chalk-filtered water from the brewery's own artesian well and most of the hops used are grown in Kent. It also still uses the UK's last remaining unlined solid oak mash tuns.

Mackesons was founded in Hythe in 1801 by two Mackeson brothers. Its fame eventually rested on its early twentieth-century introduction, Mackeson's Milk Stout, so called because milk sugar (lactose) was used in its production. Later the Mackesons sold the concern, though it retained their name, and moved on to more respectable things – one of them served in Winston Churchill's postwar cabinet and was made a baronet – but thanks to clever advertising campaigns, Mackeson's Milk Stout became a household name. Unlike Shepherd Neame, which still thrives in Faversham, the Hythe brewery site closed in 1968.

The third brewery of note was Fremlin's of Maidstone, bought by the deeply religious Ralph Fremlin in 1861. He promptly sold off all the public houses owned by the company, as he did not approve of them, and produced his beer for domestic consumption. At one time, Fremlin's was the biggest brewer in Kent, its premises dominating the Maidstone riverside, and Ralph's descendants soon accumulated a good number of tied houses and off-licenses. They were as religious as the founder, though. Until the end of the 1950s, all staff were expected to attend a nearby church on Good Friday and at Christmas. Failure to do so resulted in loss of the company Christmas turkey. The brew house closed in 1972.

Away from the public house and the church, chapel or synagogue, people began to use their increased leisure time to take part in organised sports.

Cricket was played mainly in rural areas by all classes, often with gentry rubbing shoulders with their own estate workers, for the duration of the match, at least. The first known description of the game was published in 1706, and the 'Laws of Cricket' were drawn up in 1744. They were not always followed to the letter: in 1776, a cricket match between Kent and Essex resulted in two players being shot dead and another run through with a bayonet.

In the early days, balls were delivered by being bowled underarm, until in 1822, playing for Kent, a Sutton Valence man, John Willes, bowled 'round-arm', or overarm. He had apparently developed the technique while practising with his sister Christina, who found her skirts impeded under-arm delivery. Traditionalists were appalled at such a radical innovation, and round-arm bowling was outlawed until 1835. Willes passed his skill on to

Kent County Cricket team looking rather chilly in 1913. (Author's collection)

Alfred Mynn, a Goudhurst farmer nicknamed the Lion of Kent. He was a huge man whose fast overarm action terrified pad-less and glove-less batsmen and wicketkeepers alike in a career which lasted from 1832 to 1859. The technique was also adopted by George 'Farmer' Bennett, so called because of his rustic appearance, a burglar turned bricklayer who made his debut for the county in 1853. Between 1860 and 1871 he took more than thirty wickets in a season eight times, using his unique slow overarm bowling.

Although ad hoc county teams were formed, a club was slow to develop, but in 1870, after several false starts, Kent County Cricket Club in its present form was established, and now has its headquarters in picturesque grounds in Canterbury which were bought in 1896.

Nearly every village in Kent had its team, too. As early as 1731 Chelsfield village sent a cricket team to play a match against 'London' at Kennington Common and four years later the first recorded Bromley cricket match took place on Shooting Common. Horsmonden Cricket Club has records of a match played in 1743 against the Honourable Artillery Company.

Early teams played on whatever patch of more-or-less level grass they could find. At Four Elms, a hamlet near Hever Castle, the club played on Lord Bramwell's land, next to a cabbage field. Folkestone Cricket Club, founded in the hilly town in the 1850s, sometimes played on the Leas, a clifftop site. At Eastry, they used land in front of Updown House, home of the local squire, and have continued to do so ever since. At Egerton, Lord Cornwallis generously gave the village 4.5 hectares of land for use as a recreation ground. Unfortunately, it was on a steep slope and entirely unsuitable for sport, so the village cricket and football teams carried on playing elsewhere, courtesy of local landowners and farmers, until the ground was levelled in the 1960s.

The oddest cricket ground of them all, however, was the Goodwin Sands. In the summer of 1824, Captain K. Martin, then the harbour master at Ramsgate, instituted the first known cricket match on the sands, at low water. It became a tradition. When hovercraft ran from Dover, they used to make occasional trips to the Goodwins and an annual cricket match was played until 2003. It was not without its perils. A BBC film crew, attempting to stage a reconstruction in 2006, had to be rescued by RNLI lifeboats when they ran into difficulties.

Association Football was mostly a working man's sport and in the last quarter of the nineteenth century football teams were formed all over the county. Most have been through many incarnations over the years, and only Gillingham Football Club, 'The Gills', is now a major league player. Founded as New Brompton in 1893 (the name was changed for the 1912/13 season), the club adopted professional status the following year and became a founder member of the Southern League, winning the Division Two title in 1895 and gaining promotion by beating Swindon. Thereafter, it was downhill for a number of years, until the 1940s saw the revival of the club's fortunes, which has continued to the present day and resulted in two visits to Wembley.

Probably Kent's most remarkable footballer was Walter Tull, born in Folkestone in 1888, who went from an unpromising start to become only the third black man to play first division professional football. The grandson of a slave, he was the son of a Barbadian carpenter and a Kent-born mother.

Walter Tull is commemorated in Folkestone, his birthplace, by a plaque on the side of a bandstand. Plans to erect a statue of him elsewhere have so far come to nought. (Anne Thompson)

After the deaths of both his parents he lived in a Methodist orphanage from the age of 9, but by the age of 21 was playing for Tottenham Hotspur. During the First World War he achieved another record, becoming the first black infantry officer in a regular British Army regiment. He was killed in action in France in March 1917.

For those who liked football but could not play, Peter Adolph of Langton Green near Tunbridge Wells came up with an alternative. In 1947, he created a table-top football game, the figures made from a Woolworths button from his mother's coat with a washer pushed inside. Subbuteo was born, and the game was manufactured in Tunbridge Wells until the 1980s.

Swimming as an organised sport started to become popular in the nineteenth century, too. Before the opening of the first swimming pools, rivers were used. Maidstone had probably the first swimming club in Kent, started in 1844, but the pollution of the Medway in the town forced its closure until it was able to re-open in the town swimming pool in 1895. Around this time, the Medway Swimming Club got underway in Rochester, its activities centering on a raft moored in the river. It was not until after the First World War that the club moved to the local swimming baths.

Swimming clubs also flourished at Tunbridge Wells, Canterbury and Dover, but it was Captain Matthew Webb who, on 24 August 1875, started the fashion for swimming competitively. His epic swim from Dover to Calais, well-greased with porpoise

A statue of Captain Webb on Dover seafront, supported by dolphins and seashells. He died eight years after his epic Channel swim, attempting to swim the rapids below Niagara Falls. (Anne Thompson)

oil, took him twenty-one hours to complete using breaststroke, and the changing tides meant that he actually covered a distance of 62km, rather more than the 42 he had planned. He was hailed as a hero on his return to England and was showered with gifts and money.

Before Webb's attempt, there had been some assisted Channel swims. In 1863, William Hoskins swam astride a bale of hay, and in 1875 an American, Paul Boyton, proved that it could be done wearing a life-saving suit with inflated air pockets. Webb's example led to a national spate of swimming pool construction and swimming lessons at pools. His feat was not emulated for another thirty-six years, although many tried. Then, in 1911, Thomas Burgess, smeared with lard and wearing motorcyclist's goggles and rubber trunks, did the crossing in twenty-two hours. The first woman made the swim in 1923, and the challenge became so popular that the Channel Swimming Association was set up in 1927. Since then, there have been countless races, relay swims, two-way and even three-way swims, and some swimmers have made as many as forty-three separate crossings. The fastest single crossing was achieved in 2012 with a time of six hours and fifty-five minutes.

On dry land, golf became the sport of choice of the well-heeled, and golf courses popped up all over the county. The sandy open spaces near the coast were especially suitable and the growth of the railways enabled Londoners to enjoy the facilities they offered.

The Royal St George's Golf Club at Sandwich was the first of the coastal sites, opening in 1887, and was to all intents and purposes a London club with its green at the seaside. All the committee meetings were held in London until the turn of the century when a local secretary was engaged. To help commuters, a special tram service was laid on from Sandwich station to the club. It has been the venue for the Open Championship on fourteen occasions since 1894, and was granted royal status in 1902 by Edward VII. In 1927, the Prince of Wales (later Edward VIII) was Club Captain. A keen golfer, he also played the Sene Valley course, near Hythe, with Sir Philip Sassoon who lived at nearby Port Lympne. Always very traditional, Royal St George's only admitted women members in 2015, and the dress code remains strict. Its rules state that on the course, clothing 'may include the wearing of tailored golf shorts but, for men, only with long socks with a turnover top'.

Most of the coastal clubs suffered during the course of two world wars when the shoreline was heavily fortified and under attack. The second golf club at Sandwich, Prince's, had a rifle range built on it during the First World War. At St Augustine's at Pegwell Bay, a tank trap laid during the Second World War was later converted into a water hazard across the course and the dip in the first fairway is the end result of a bomb crater. Walmer and Kingsdown golf course was covered in barbed-wire entanglements and could not re-open until 1948 and the Sene Valley course was heavily damaged by German bombs and shells, and a direct hit wiped out an entire anti-aircraft crew based there. Then, in 1953, during the terrifying east coast storm surge, Prince's and the Whitstable and Seasalter course were inundated with up to 2.5m of sea water.

A day of sporting activities might end with a trip to the theatre, or for the less culturally minded, the music hall or later the cinema. By the nineteenth century, most Kent towns of any size had at least one venue where the performing arts could be enjoyed.

Dover's theatrical connections go back at least to the days of William Shakespeare when the Bard's company, The King's Men, visited the town. At the time, he was writing *King Lear* and it was Dover's Hay Cliff that apparently gave him the inspiration for the scene in the play when the blinded Earl of Gloucester remarks how 'horrible steep' is the walk up the cliff. It is still horrible steep but is now known as the Shakespeare Cliff.

The town had venues catering for every taste. In 1785, the Fector banking family opened a small theatre in the town's Snargate Street with a production of *The Siege of Damascus*, but before long it was rivalled by a larger establishment, part of Robert Copeland's string of theatres, which included venues in Deal, Sandwich and later Margate. An astute businessman, Copeland negotiated a deal giving his Dover premises a Royal prefix, approved by the Duke of Clarence, later William IV. It later became a music hall, joining the Alhambra Music Hall which opened in the Market Square in 1864.

Sandgate's theatrical venue started, as many did, as a hall built onto the back of a public house. In 1858, the landlord of the Bricklayers Arms built at the rear of his premises a new room 20m by 8m, lit by chandeliers, which was used as a music hall. It was later renamed the Alhambra and in 1875, a 'singing mouse' appeared on the playbill. Later, the soon to be deceased

Belle Elmore, the wife of the notorious murderer Dr Crippen, performed there.

At Chatham, Charles Barnard bought the Railway Tavern in 1852 and added a concert hall to it. It thrived for nearly thirty years, and when it was destroyed by fire, a Palace of Varieties, seating over 1,000 with two houses a night, was built in its place. The success of this music hall enabled the Barnard family to build a playhouse, showing more highbrow productions. It opened in 1899 with a production of *The Liars*, a comedy of manners.

In the early twentieth century films, 'moving pictures', started to become available to music hall owners. They were, for the most part, short documentaries of fifteen or twenty minutes, not long enough to fill an entire evening performance, and so were shown alongside a programme of variety acts.

At Gravesend, the general-purpose Public Hall was used for film shows from 1908. That year, audiences were treated to *Wilbur Wright's Aeroplane in Full Flight*, *The Kaiser Reviewing German Army Troops* and *The Gordon Highlanders and Bengal Cavalry in Calcutta*. Nine years later, when full-length feature films were coming out of Hollywood, the first dedicated cinemas started to appear, and the Gravesend Palace Cinema opened its doors, providing silent film showings accompanied by an orchestra and pianist. By 1933, it had become the Super Cinema with a Compton organ rising from the pit on a lift. The film star Anna Neagle made a personal appearance for the opening, which showed the film *Cavalcade*. Admission cost from 4d up to 1s 10d and even at this late date, there were still variety acts and organ interludes.

The scenario was the same elsewhere, as music halls and theatres adapted to the new craze for the movies. The Alhambra at Sandgate was reopened as Sandgate Picture Palace and in June 1930 showed talkies for the first time. It finally closed in 1951. At Dover, the Royal Hippodrome still produced variety shows but had moving pictures as an occasional feature. It carried on until 1941 when a direct hit from a German shell ended its days. The first purpose-built cinema in the town, the King's Hall, opened in 1911, seating 800 and was followed by seven others. Now, none remain.

The seaside resorts of Kent also began to take advantage of a changing and expanding market. Sea bathing remained popular and people were beginning to enjoy paddling and swimming in the sea, rather than regarding the exercise as purely therapeutic. Bathing machines started to fall out of favour as too restrictive, and now that bathing costumes were on show on the beach, most resorts introduced strict rules as to what should be worn while taking a dip. Hythe's by-laws, drawn up in 1912, were typical. Everyone over the age of 10 had to wear 'an opaque costume reaching from the shoulders to within three inches of the knee to prevent indecent exposure of the person'. In case this was not enough to spare delicate sensibilities, most beaches had 'ladies only' bathing areas until well into the twentieth century.

Resorts responded to rising demand by offering a variety of accommodation. Local people let out rooms, and lodging houses burgeoned. Margate, in particular, went all-out to attract working-class visitors with a range of leisure opportunities including, in 1866, a music hall, the Hall by the Sea.

Cardow's Cadets were a favourite of genteel Folkestone audiences, performing a variety act of song and comedy at the Red Roof Chalet next to the Bathing Establishment from 1905 until the late 1920s. (Author's collection)

It was later bought by George Sanger, a circus owner, who used the surrounding land to build an amusement park, with a mock ruined abbey, lake, statues and a menagerie, as well as sideshows and roundabouts. For a short time, there was even a skating rink. During the early part of the twentieth century, the site was developed into a successful tourist attraction, Dreamland, with rollercoasters, a cinema, a lido and a ballroom. Elsewhere in the resort, the Hippodrome, a theatre with a seating capacity of nearly 2,000 was opened in 1898. Its first production was the appropriately named musical farce, *The Shop Girl*.

The first Kent holiday camps started to develop not long after the First World War, in Dymchurch. They began as tented camps for children run by the Boys' Brigade, with the philanthropic motive of getting them out of the unhealthy atmosphere of London. The Brigade then bought disused land and accommodation from the RAF, but unable to manage it successfully, they sold the whole complex to a developer, who turned it into Dymchurch Holiday Camp. The concept would become the leisure success story of the mid-twentieth century.

Folkestone, on the other hand, deliberately deterred the lower orders and the day-tripper. The town's principal landowner was Lord Radnor, who had a vision of Folkestone as a 'superior' resort, and the coming of the railway and the new cross-Channel service gave economic impetus to his plans. Wide streets and squares were laid out and splendid hotels built. Newly built houses were large, to accommodate well-to-do families with several servants. Civic pride was expressed in the showy new town hall, built in 1861. Lord Radnor also owned the Leas, a broad, grassy clifftop sward to the west of the town, which offered unrivalled sea views. Fine lawns and flowerbeds were laid out there, with walkways and bandstands, and there were lifts, using a water-balance system, to and from the beach below. Folkestone became a fashionable and select resort, which attracted the retired, invalids and people of independent means.

Eleven

'THERE IS NOTHING PERMANENT EXCEPT CHANGE'[1]

In 1900, despite the efforts of the Chartists in the nineteenth century, only about two-thirds of men in the UK could vote. No woman could. The Chartist campaign, demanding a vote for every man, was not particularly well-supported in southern England, although a group of Crayford printers espoused the cause and William Cuffay, the Chatham-born son of a freed slave, became president of the London Chartists. The campaign for women's suffrage started 1866, and several Kent towns had petitioned Parliament in favour of the campaign, Folkestone, Tonbridge and Ramsgate among them, but by the turn of the century some campaigners were frustrated by the lack of progress made through peaceable means. Mrs Pankhurst's Women's Social and Political Union (WSPU) advocated a more militant approach. In 1906, the *Daily Mail* coined the name 'Suffragette' to describe these radical women. It was not a term of endearment.

Women's suffrage groups were well represented in Kent, with Tonbridge and Sevenoaks having particularly strong memberships. Taking advantage of crowds of visitors, open-air meetings were held on the beaches at Margate, Broadstairs and Cliftonville in summer 1909. The next year Emmeline Pankhurst herself visited Canterbury and Thanet, and her daughter Christabel spoke at Herne Bay and Folkestone. But there was also a large anti-suffrage movement in Kent, and the local press was mostly hostile. In 1910, WSPU flags were torn down in Walmer, and a group of Gravesend women attempting to hold an open-air meeting were set on by a 1,000-strong crowd, who threw orange peel and 'other missiles'.

1 Heraclitus, 435 BC – 475 BC.

Some suffragettes paid dearly for their activism. Georgina Cheffins of Hythe and Helen McRae of Edenbridge were both sentenced to four months in prison for breaking windows in London. Both went on hunger strike in Holloway and were forcibly fed, a degrading and painful experience. Cheffins, undeterred, returned to Hythe, where she lived with a fellow-WSPU member and set up a suffrage shop in the High Street.

The suffragettes' particular *bête noire* was Herbert Asquith, Chancellor of the Exchequer from 1906 to 1908 and then Prime Minister, a man strongly opposed to women's suffrage. Suffragettes lost no opportunity to harass him. In September 1909, three Kent women spent a weekend doing just that. Asquith was staying at Lympne Castle. On Sunday morning he attended church, but on leaving was accosted by the trio, one of whom allegedly hit him repeatedly. That afternoon he went to play golf at nearby Littlestone. The women were there, too, but were removed. They then went to Hythe and somehow acquired a boat which they rowed along the Royal Military Canal to below Lympne Castle, climbed, in the dark, the steep wooded slope and threw two stones through Asquith's dining room window as he sat with guests, shouting: 'That is what the women of England think of you.'

In 1913, the women turned their attention to Kent County Cricket Club's grounds at Tunbridge Wells, which had a policy of non-admittance to women. They started a fire in the dressing rooms, which completely destroyed the pavilion. In front of the smoking remains, firemen found suffragette literature and a picture of Emmeline Pankhurst. Sir Arthur Conan Doyle, addressing a local meeting of anti-suffragists, said that the act was like 'blowing up a blind man and his dog'.

The outbreak of hostilities on 2 August 1914 put a temporary end to the struggle as the suffragettes diverted their energies to the war effort. Kent had not been in the front line for over a hundred years, and this time was different. There was no great fear of invasion – the Kaiser's forces were too bogged down in the trenches of northern France, but what was new was the use of aircraft to bring the war to the homes and workplaces of ordinary people. The invention of powered flight revolutionised many aspects of life in the twentieth century, and Kent was witness to some of its earliest triumphs – and disasters.

A plaque on Dover seafront marking the achievement of Charles Rolls. Together with Henry Royce, he founded the Rolls-Royce car manufacturing firm. (Anne Thompson)

Orville Wright had made the first short flight in 1903. Longer trips soon became feasible and in 1909 the British newspaper magnate Lord Northcliffe offered a prize of £1,000 to the first person to fly across the English Channel. An attempt by Hubert Latham resulted in the first ever landing of an aircraft on a body of water, when he had engine trouble over the English Channel. Another contender damaged his machine in practice, so it was Louis Bleriot who, on 25 July 1909, claimed the money. His journey took him thirty-seven minutes and his landing not far from Dover Castle smashed his propeller and undercarriage, but he emerged unscathed.

The next year, Charles Rolls flew from Dover to Calais and back in a single flight. He was killed a month later during a flying display at Bournemouth, thus achieving another record, that of being the first Briton to die in a plane crash.

The outbreak of war led to a surge in the development of all sorts of aircraft, as their potential for fighting was recognised. The extraordinary Short brothers led the field with their workshops in Kent: Horace on the Isle of Sheppey with aeroplanes and Oswald in Rochester with seaplanes. Another brother, Eustace, built balloons and airships in Battersea.

The Royal Naval Air Service, a forerunner of the RAF, set up seaplane stations on the Isle of Grain and at Westgate. Airship stations were located at Capel-le-Ferne near Dover and at Kingsnorth near Rochester. In Thanet, an airstrip was created at Manston, and eight training airfields were established across the county to instruct new pilots. They were in constant demand to replace those lost – the mortality rate among fliers was disastrously high.

The first ever air raid on mainland England occurred in Dover on Christmas Eve 1914, when a single German bomb was dropped near Dover Castle. It landed in a garden, made a small crater and knocked the gardener out of a tree he was pruning. In fact, the bomb was thrown rather than dropped. The pilot had to lift the bomb with both hands while holding his joystick steady between his knees, and lob it over the side of the plane without falling out himself.

The Germans soon realised that air raids on English soil would damage morale and may shorten the war. Zeppelin airships could easily reach London with a sizeable bombload, but they were slow, so Gotha bombers were used as well. Kent was not spared, especially when poor visibility meant that primary targets could not be found and the deadly cargo was simply jettisoned before the English Channel.

The second raid on Kent was in 1915, at Faversham and Sittingbourne, and raids continued sporadically throughout 1916. By 1918, Dover had experienced 113 attacks from the air, but the single most destructive raid was in Folkestone on 25 May 1917. Twenty-three Gotha bombers, unable to find their London targets in thick cloud, turned south, following the railway line to the Channel ports. They dropped bombs en route, including at the Ashford railway works and the army camp at Shorncliffe, killing several civilians and eighteen soldiers. Folkestone was almost their last chance to dispose of their bombs before the sea crossing. They reached it at about 6.30 p.m. on that warm spring evening. A rumour had spread that potatoes were at last available at a town centre greengrocer's and women were patiently queuing inside the shop and in the street while their children played nearby. The shop took a direct hit and sixty-one were killed.

The bombers flew on to Dover, but they met resistance from gun batteries and three planes of the Royal Naval Air Service, and abandoned the mission. Others would follow and early warning and defence became priorities.

When incoming raiders were reported, Royal Flying Corps and Royal Naval Air Service planes took off from airfields across the county and anti-aircraft batteries around Chatham Dockyard and the navy's depot on the Isle of Grain were put on alert. In the first years of the war, warning systems relied on observers, but experiments were started with acoustic detection. Some involved a device that resembled a cluster of hearing trumpets, but 'sound mirrors' were found to be more effective. The first was a simple concave dish, 4.5m in diameter carved into the cliffs near Dover. Later, larger concrete models were erected at vulnerable sites on the coast. These devices had a metal pole in the centre with a microphone attached. The mirror worked by focusing the noise of aircraft engines onto the micro-phone, which amplified the sound. The relatively slow aircraft of the time could be heard and located well before they came into sight.

The war had a profound effect on the county. Some industries expanded rapidly: the Vickers armaments works at Crayford, Erith and Dartford; the naval dockyard at Chatham; and the munitions factories at Faversham, where young women replaced the male workers who had joined the ser-vices. They were known as 'munitionettes', or 'canary girls', as the TNT they worked with turned their skin yellow.

A surviving sound mirror near West Hythe. Nine metres in diameter, it is constructed of metal mesh, supported by an angle-iron frame and covered with concrete. There is a listening chamber underneath. (Anne Thompson)

On Sunday 2 April 1916, fire broke out at one of the Faversham munitions works, the Cotton Powder Company. Before it could be evacuated, 15 tonnes of TNT and 150 tonnes of ammonium nitrate exploded. The blast caused damage over a huge area, including broken windows as far away as Southend. Its effects were so destructive that the true death toll will never be known, but it was probably about 110 men, including the entire Gunpowder Works Fire Brigade, local firemen and ambulance men. None of the canary girls was killed: Sunday was their rest day.

During these war years, the coastal towns of Kent became accustomed to the constant movement of people to and from the continent, starting in 1914 with the influx of 60,000 Belgian refugees through Folkestone, many of whom were initially helped and accommodated locally. Then came the movement of troops and supplies between France and England. It has been estimated that 10 million troops passed through Folkestone harbour, the

Tuner Prize winner Mark Wallinger's *Folk Stones* on the Leas at Folkestone. Individually numbered stones (19,240 in total) stand for the exact number of British soldiers killed on 1 July 1916, most of whom would have passed through this port. (Anne Thompson)

main embarkation port for France, on their way to, or returning from, the Western Front. The rumble of guns in France could clearly be heard in the south of the county and, during the first days of the Battle of the Somme in 1916, as far away as Sevenoaks.

Kent became used to foreign accents, not just from Belgian refugees, but from troops from across the British Empire. There were up to 50,000 Canadian soldiers stationed at Shorncliffe Camp at any given time from 1915 to 1918, waiting to travel to the front – the place was said to have become a suburb of Toronto. Relations between local people and the military were generally very good, and even today, at the Shorncliffe military cemetery, an annual Canada Day ceremony is held in remembrance of those who passed through the camp but did not return home. One of them was Lietenant-Colonel John McRae, author of the poem 'In Flanders Field'.

Local people would have been less aware of the presence of the Chinese

Labour Corps at the camp: they were segregated and heavily chaperoned. They had been recruited to fill the manpower shortage caused by heavy losses in France, and were mostly poor farmers attracted by the bounty on signing up of 15 Chinese dollars. Their work was menial and ill-paid and when the war ended some were used for mine clearance, or to recover the bodies of soldiers and fill in miles of trenches.

Tucked away in a corner of Shorncliffe military cemetery are half-a-dozen graves of members of the Chinese Labour Corps. The Chinese script tells us that he came from Pingdu city in Shandong. (Author's collection)

Equally mysterious to the public was the secret port by the banks of the River Stour near the Roman fort of Richborough. Built to service the British Expeditionary Force with its logistics, including ammunition, tanks, horses, rations and fuel, it was the starting point of a ferry service to northern France. Most of the equipment and arms for the Ypres Salient were sent across from Richborough Port, using sea-going barges and the very first roll-on roll-off ferries.

The end of the war did not bring peace for all. A 1918 Act of Parliament gave all men over 21, and some women, the right to vote, but the 'land fit for heroes' promised by the wartime coalition government did not materialise. Instead, there was widespread economic depression. Kent, lacking heavy manufacturing, suffered less than the rest of the country, and even developed its own new industry, coal mining.

In 1880, the first attempts to build a Channel tunnel at the Shakespeare Cliff in Dover had been brought to a halt when the government of the day got cold feet about the national security implications of a direct link with France. The developers used their workforce instead to investigate rumours that there was coal underground there, and struck lucky. In 1896, Arthur Burr set up the first Kent coal company, but the site proved unprofitable, and a syndicate headed by him turned its attentions to the villages of Snowdown and Tilmanstone, where productive pits were in operation by 1913. They were followed by another at Chislet in 1919 and Betteshanger, where excavations reached coal in 1927.

There were great hopes for this new coalfield, but even at its peak in 1935 it accounted for less than 1 per cent of UK coal output. Kent coal was difficult to extract and its excellent quality made it the most expensive in the country. The pits also suffered from a chronic labour shortage. Mining was new to the county and there were no local experienced workers. They were poached instead from traditional mining areas such as Wales, Scotland, Durham and Yorkshire by the inducement of higher wages. The inducement was needed because working conditions were grim. Snowdown, the deepest pit, was reputedly the worst in the country. Such was the heat and humidity underground it was nicknamed 'the hell hole'. Miners there worked naked, save for a belt and boots, drinking around 15 litres of water during their shift, and heat exhaustion was common.

A statue entitled *The Waiting Miner* at the entrance to the country park, near the former Betteshanger Colliery, near Deal. (Anne Thompson)

The miners were often treated with hostile suspicion by locals, just as the hoppers had been. Their strange accents and coal-blackened faces set them apart. Signs saying 'No Miners' soon appeared in shops and pubs. Accommodation, when it was built for them, was in separate pit villages, developed in isolated rural sites or well outside the main residential areas of towns.

Meanwhile, developments in Germany were leading inexorably to another world war. In November 1938, the Nazis in Germany and Austria rounded up 30,000 Jewish men and sent them to concentration camps. In response, the British Government allowed the Central Fund for German Jewry to set up an operation to save some of them, an operation identical to the *Kindertransport*, in which the men would be brought to Dover and housed in a transit camp near Richborough before they moved on. A First World War camp there, the Kitchener Camp, became the temporary home of 4,000 German-speaking, mostly single, Jewish men.

They started arriving in February 1939, and continued until the outbreak of war in September. The exercise was not without its problems, as Lady Grace Pearson, a Sandwich dignitary, was also president of the local British Union of Fascists. However, she was apparently widely disliked by the ordinary citizenry, and the town generally welcomed the new arrivals. The men were encouraged to volunteer for the British Army in the Pioneer Corps, and many did, fighting with the British Expeditionary Force in France.

The camp was closed in 1940, and the remaining men dispersed to other parts of the UK or to America.

The first months of the Second World War must have seemed to the county very much like a resumption of the hostilities of the First World War, with troops leaving the Channel ports for France in their thousands and fortifications appearing on the coast. Then in May 1940, Hitler invaded Holland, Belgium and France, isolating Allied forces on the beaches at Dunkirk.

From a military base in the tunnels beneath Dover Castle, Vice-Admiral Bertram Ramsey instigated Operation Dynamo to evacuate as many as possible, and the rescue mission later called 'a miracle' by Winston Churchill started. The beach at Dunkirk was on a shallow slope, so no large vessel could approach. An appeal was made for smaller boats to go to the beaches and ferry the men to larger vessels or to bring them back across the Channel. More than 700 of the legendary 'little ships' answered the call and assembled at Sheerness Dockyard to await orders, among them lifeboats, fishing smacks, dredgers, trawlers, drifters, tugs, even a mudhopper. They sailed at 2200 on 29 May, crewed by volunteers, some of whom had never been to sea before: factory workers from Gravesend, air-raid wardens, dockyard employees.

Over the next week, under constant shelling and bombing, the little ships and their bigger sisters brought home a total of 338,226 Allied troops, including French and Polish soldiers. One, a paddle steamer named the *Medway Queen*, made seven return trips saving over 7,000 lives. Most of the ships berthed at Dover or Ramsgate, where special trains were laid on to take the exhausted men to London. They stopped briefly en route at Headcorn in the Weald of Kent, where the village women worked day and night in shifts to provide tea and sandwiches. Defeat had been turned into a kind of victory.

Two months later, Hitler launched Operation Sea Lion. His objective was to invade England with twenty divisions landing between Ramsgate and Lyme Regis. Detailed plans were laid for the invasion, but their success depended on the elimination of Britain's air power. The Battle of Britain, fought in the skies over the farms, orchards and villages of Kent, started in July 1940 and lasted for fifteen dramatic weeks. German Messerschmitts, Dorniers and Stukas fought against British Hurricanes, Spitfires and Defiants from airfields at Biggin Hill, Manston and Hawkinge. There

Hawkinge cemetery, next to the site of the former Second World War airfield, has a section reserved for German aircrew who lost their lives in the skies over Kent. (Author's collection)

were dogfights involving 200 or more planes over Dover and Ashford; the Short's aircraft factory, still functioning at Rochester, was bombed; incendiary bombs killed thirty-one in Ramsgate and twenty in Gillingham. All the RAF's airfields were bombed repeatedly. The countryside was littered with crashed fighter planes and German bombers.

On 15 September 1940, now celebrated as Battle of Britain Day, a huge Luftwaffe force, more than 3km wide, crossed the Kent coast at Dungeness. Twenty-three RAF squadrons were scrambled to meet it. The Germans were repelled, but a second wave, just as large, flew in during the afternoon. Again, they met with determined resistance and that night the public was informed that Fighter Command had shot down 183 German aircraft. In fact, the real figure was fifty-six, but the exaggeration was a huge boost to morale, and the damage to the Luftwaffe was more than just lost aircraft. Although the Battle of Britain lasted until October, that one day ensured that Operation Sea Lion was dead in the water.

The war, however, was far from over. The corner of Kent nearest to the French coast soon acquired the name 'Hellfire Corner' and Dover became the country's front-line town. The town was pounded with bombs and shells for four years. Hundreds of civilians and servicemen and women were killed, with thousands of buildings damaged across the district. The very last shell fell on Dover on 26 September 1944 at 7.15 p.m. on an umbrella manufacturer's shop.

The townspeople took refuge in the tunnels beneath the castle. They were cold, damp and unventilated, but relatively safe, and some of the population slept there for years. They were not alone. In Chislehurst, 8,000 people sheltered from air raids in an underground cave city; at Ramsgate, former railway tunnels 20m below ground were used; and at Rochester at the Short Brothers' site, a complete new factory was built underground.

Even after the D-Day landings, the attacks continued when the Germans started launching flying bombs – nicknamed doodlebugs – from northern France. Sixty-four landed in Kent. The first victim was Benenden, a small Wealden village. The next week, forty-seven soldiers were killed at Charing Heath. A huge anti-aircraft battery was set up along the coast and another on the ridge of the North Downs, supplemented by 2,000 barrage balloons. Off the Kent coast three army forts in the Thames estuary shot down thirty doodlebugs headed for London. The forts, whose remains can still be seen, each consisted of seven separate towers linked by walkways. Each tower comprised an octagonal 'house' on four hollow concrete legs, 19m high. As well as anti-aircraft functions, the forts also provided an accurate radar service.

In Europe, the Allied troops needed petrol to maintain their advance towards Germany. This was supplied from Kent via PLUTO – Pipe Line Under The Ocean. A pipeline from Dungeness to Boulogne enabled 15,900 litres of petrol to be pumped across the Channel. A network of pipes over 1,600km long linked Dungeness to ports in the West Country and refineries such as the Isle of Grain, and PLUTO's tubes, each weighing 15 tonnes, were manufactured in Gravesend and welded together at Littlestone, then towed out to sea by tugs. More pipelines followed, and by February 1945 nearly half a million litres of petrol a day were being delivered.

Recovery in Kent after the war was, as in the rest of the country, slow, but closer links with Europe and the growth of trade gave impetus to develop-

In 1983, it was still possible to walk through the extant section of the abandoned 1970s Channel Tunnel. (Author's collection)

ment of better, faster ways of crossing the Channel. As early as 1926, the Southern Railway had introduced its iconic Golden Arrow train, entirely comprising luxurious Pullman cars, but passengers still had to disembark at Dover to take the ferry. In 1934, the first train ferry was put into service at the port, designed to carry twelve sleeping cars and two baggage vans. This, the Night Ferry, was the first through service from London to Paris and made the journey from Victoria Station to the Gare du Nord in eleven hours.

The Night Ferry continued to run until 1980, but meanwhile the growth of car ownership meant that there was competition to find faster ways to deliver motorists to France for their holidays. Dover's docks were unsuitable for the huge growth in roll-on roll-off traffic, so a new Eastern Docks terminal was constructed under the White Cliffs in the 1960s.

The ferries soon had competition from the hovercraft, invented by Sir Christopher Cockerell, which made its maiden cross-Channel 'flight' on 25 July 1959, fifty years to the day after Bleriot's historic journey. In 1966, a regular service was offered to passengers from Pegwell Bay, near Ramsgate, to Calais and two years later a service from Dover to Calais started. The crossing, in good weather, was undoubtedly fast at only thirty minutes, but was noisy, cramped, and, in rough seas, very, very uncomfortable. The hovercraft could carry only fifty-two cars, and the competitive edge of their speed was seriously undermined by the building of the Channel Tunnel. The service ended in 2000.

After the first Channel Tunnel excavations of the late nineteenth century were abandoned, hostile relations with other European countries meant that the idea was not re-examined until the 1970s. In 1973, Edward Heath for the UK and Georges Pompidou for France signed a treaty to build a tunnel, but Harold Wilson, the next British prime minister, stopped the work in 1975, when costs started to spiral.

Ten years later, a proposal for a tunnel, based on the 1970s model, was accepted by both the French and British governments. The treaty agreeing the scheme was signed in Canterbury Cathedral in 1986 and work started on the UK side the next year. In 1990, the historic breakthrough was made as French and British tunnelers met under the sea, 22km from Kent and 15.5 from France. For the first time in 8,000 years, it was possible to walk, or at least drive, from England to France. In 1994, freight, car and passenger train services started to use the tunnel, and in 2007, with the opening of the High Speed Train service from St Pancras, it was possible to travel by rail from London to Paris in two and a quarter hours.

The race to provide ever-faster Channel crossings was a cause, in part, of the tragedy of the *Herald of Free Enterprise*. The modern eight-deck car and passenger ferry had been designed for rapid loading and unloading on the competitive route, and there were no watertight compartments. When the ship left Zeebrugge on the night of 6 March 1987 bound for Dover, her bow-door was left open. The sea immediately flooded the decks, and within minutes she was lying on her side in shallow water. Two hundred and five people died. A coroner's inquest returned verdicts of unlawful killing.

Seven people involved at the company were charged with gross negligence and manslaughter, and the operating company, P&O, was charged with corporate manslaughter. The case eventually collapsed but it did set a precedent that corporate manslaughter is legally admissible in English courts. Since the disaster, improvements have been made to the design of car ferries, with watertight ramps, indicators showing the position of the bow-doors, and the banning of undivided decks.

Freight traffic was one of the beneficiaries of faster, easier Channel crossings, and would-be illegal immigrants into the UK began to take advantage of the constant flow. Hiding inside or underneath trucks, secreting themselves on trains or even walking through the tunnel, they risked their lives to make the journey. The controversial camp set up by the French Red Cross at Sangatte near Calais to accommodate the refugees was closed in 2002, but new, informal encampments continue to spring up in the area and attempts to cross the Channel clandestinely continue unabated.

Faster transport links meant that the world was shrinking, and Kent was shrinking, too – literally. Following the loss of Greenwich and Woolwich in 1889, Bromley, Beckenham, Penge, Orpington and Chislehurst became part of Greater London in 1965. The county changed in other ways. Farming, once so important to the economy, has been in decline since the 1950s. During the world wars, Kent farmers fed the nation, producing wagonloads of apples and pears, gallons of beer and tons of cereal crops, but

outbreaks of BSE, the so-called mad cow disease, first identified in cattle in 1986, and foot and mouth, the most recent in 2007, have challenged the industry. To survive, many farms have diversified, becoming tourist destinations, craft shops, or even ice cream factories.

Other industries closed or moved on. The Short Brothers factory at

These mounted train wheels in New Town are all that remain of the huge Ashford railway works. (Anne Thompson)

Rochester, which had produced Sunderland seaplanes and Stirling bombers for the RAF, moved its operation to Belfast in 1948. The Ashford railway works shut in 1983. In the days of steam, it had built the great locomotives needed, but the switch to diesel and then to electricity ended the need for many of the heavy engineering skills. With the loss of nearly 1,000 jobs, the closure was a huge setback for the town, but six years later it was chosen as the site for a new international rail terminal for Eurostar trains to the continent. This, together with a business park next to the new M20 motorway, guaranteed the town's continued, indeed improved, prosperity.

Chatham Dockyard closed 1984 with the loss of 7,000 jobs. Chatham-built ships had fought in every English war from the battles against the Spanish Armada to the Falklands, and construction had evolved from wood and sail through iron and steam to destroyers and nuclear submarines. The last nuclear submarine to be refitted, HMS *Churchill*, and the last frigate, HMS *Hermione*, left the dockyard in 1983. The old naval base was split into three parts – the historic docks tourist attraction, the working port and a residential development on St Mary's Island. It is also home to a new university campus and a shopping outlet. Still in existence at the dockyard is the ropery – a 400m-long building where naval rope has been made commercially since 1618 – and the authentic cobbled streets, industrial buildings and Georgian and Victorian architecture have regularly been used as backdrops for film and television productions including *Les Misérables* and *Sherlock Holmes*.

When the mining industry was nationalised in 1947, the new National Coal Board started making plans to close unprofitable Kent pits. Chislet, near Canterbury, went first in 1969. By the 1980s, supported by the government, the Board was determined to make the coal industry viable by closing all the pits it deemed to be uneconomic. The National Union of Mineworkers argued that, in fact, it was bad management and poor investment which were holding the industry back. Things came to a head in 1984 when the NUM called for a national strike. The miners in Kent were the first, along with Yorkshire, to walk out, and the strike lasted for almost a year, characterised by bitterness, violence and privation and creating arguably the most serious constitutional crisis to face the prime minister, Margaret Thatcher. The Kent miners were the last to return to work, but when it was over, neither side fully recovered. Snowdown and Tilmanstone collieries closed with little opposition in 1987. Betteshanger was the last colliery in Kent, closing in 1989, just a year short of the centenary of the discovery of coal in the county. The effect on mining communities of the strike and closures was devastating.

Kent's frontline status over hundreds of years meant that there was a fairly constant military presence in the county, and this continued for a while after the Second World War, with many regiments becoming well-regarded members of local communities. The deaths of ten young Royal Marine musicians in Deal in 1989, killed by an IRA bomb, shocked the whole town, which turned out *en masse* for their funeral. The Marines, who had been given the freedom of the town, left Deal in 1996 after 130 years. The Small Arms School at Hythe, founded in 1853, closed in 1969. Barracks at Canterbury and Chatham have been cut back. However, in 2000, Folkestone welcomed the Royal Gurkha Rifles to the town, where they have one of the biggest Ghurka bases in the country. When an earthquake brought devastation to their country, Nepal, in 2015, local people joined them in mourning and in fund-raising for relief efforts.

Kent people have made history for thousands of years. Change will continue, and more history will be made, and Kent's people will rise to the challenges and take up the opportunities offered by modern life. There is, after all, little that can happen that the county has not seen, and dealt with, before.

TWELVE KENT LIVES

Kent has produced its fair share of notable men and women, some whose stories have already been told. Here is a dozen more, from all walks of life, who across the centuries called Kent home.

John Aspinall, zookeeper

John Aspinall, who made a very lucrative living as a bookmaker and professional gambler, had as a student become interested in wildlife through the unlikely medium of Rider Haggard novels. In his first home, in London's Eaton Place, he indulged his passion by keeping a capuchin monkey, a tiger cub and two Himalayan brown bears, but the unsuitability of the animals' accommodation was obvious and a fortuitous gambling windfall led to his purchase, in 1956, of Howletts, a Palladian mansion with a park of nearly 30 hectares near Canterbury. Here he established his own private zoo.

Eighteen years later, his growing collection needed yet more space, and he bought Port Lympne, a decaying mansion with 250 hectares of land near Hythe. Elephants and rhinoceroses were the first to take up residence in the new zoo. Aspinall then embarked on a ten-year project to restore the house and gardens. The extensive terraced flower beds were fertilised with 180 tonnes of readily available elephant dung.

He opened Howletts to the public in 1975, and Port Lympne Zoo the next year. Neither ever made a profit. By 1996, they contained between them over 1,000 animals, and cost £4 million a year to run, of which charges to the public contributed only £330,000.

The zoos are known for being unorthodox, and have been dogged by controversy. Aspinall's philosophy was to encourage keepers to come into close contact with potentially dangerous animals and to build up close relationships with them, as he did himself. Five animal keepers were killed by their charges in twenty years, and there were occasional maulings.

The zoos have, however, had huge success with their breeding programmes, including raising gorillas, snow leopards, Siberian tigers and black rhinos. At both sites, all the animals have large paddocks and are fed a varied diet and there is an emphasis on reducing boredom by providing a 'natural' environment, encouraging innate behaviour. Aspinall was among the first to return species to the wild, and in 1999, the year before he died, his project successfully introduced captive-bred gorillas to their ancestral home in the Congo. The Aspinall Foundation now carries on this back-to-the-wild programme, and funds animal protection projects around the world.

Sir Winston Churchill, politician and statesman

In 1908, the 32-year-old MP, former army officer and ex-war correspondent Winston Leonard Spencer-Churchill married Clementine Hozier in Westminster. Fourteen years later, as the parents of four children, they bought the house that would be their home until Churchill's death in 1965, Chartwell near Westerham.

The origins of the house lie in the sixteenth century, when Henry VIII is reputed to have stayed there during his courtship of Anne Boleyn at nearby Hever Castle. The original farmhouse was enlarged and modified during the nineteenth century. The National Trust, which now owns the property, describe it as being at that time an example of 'Victorian architecture at its least attractive, a ponderous red brick country mansion of tile-hung gables and poky oriel windows'.

It was the views across the Weald of Kent which entranced Churchill, and he employed architect Philip Tilden to modernise and extend the house. He transformed it, simplifying the design and letting in light. There were up-to-date amenities: five baths, fourteen lavatories and several telephones. Clementine Churchill oversaw the decoration.

Now out of government, Churchill designed the gardens himself. They were terraced and linked by steps descending to lakes that Churchill created by installing a series of small dams. He involved himself whole-heartedly in the project, 'wallowing in the filthiest black mud you ever saw'. In 1924, he became Chancellor of the Exchequer, and Chartwell saw many political and financial gatherings, but by the 1930s, Churchill was in the political wilderness. His views that Mussolini and Hitler threatened the peace of Europe were ignored and ridiculed, but at Chartwell Churchill developed his own intelligence network, and the stream of visitors bringing information and statistics turned the house into 'a little Foreign Office'. Meanwhile, Churchill painted, took up bricklaying (he built the brick wall around the kitchen garden) and fed his fish in the lakes.

His political isolation ended with the outbreak of the Second World War, but the proximity of Chartwell to the English Channel and the highly vis-

The statue of Churchill at Westerham, erected shortly after his death, rests on a base of Yugoslavian stone, the gift of Marshall Tito. (Anne Thompson)

ible target offered by the lakes made it susceptible to German bombers. The Churchills rarely used it until peace returned.

Chartwell was not just a family home. It was where Churchill wrote, often the sole means he had of generating an income. Here he finished his history of the First World War, *The World Crisis*, and a sequel, *The Aftermath*; a biography of his ancestor, *Marlborough*; and his memoirs of the Second World War.

It was an expensive house to maintain, and was bought by a group of Churchill's friends in 1946, with the Churchills paying a nominal rent. On Churchill's death in 1965, the house was presented to the National Trust.

Joseph Conrad, author

The Polish-born novelist Joseph Conrad lived in Kent for twenty-five years. Although English was Conrad's second language, he is regarded as one of the greatest writers in the language. His novels include *Lord Jim*, *Heart of Darkness*, *Nostromo* and *The Secret Agent*.

To escape the turmoil of his home country, his family sent him to France, where he joined the merchant navy, later switching to service on British ships and rising through the ranks to become captain. In 1886, he became a British citizen. In 1894, aged 36, Conrad reluctantly gave up the sea, partly because of poor health, partly due to the unavailability of ships, and partly because he had become so fascinated with writing that he had decided on a literary career. His first novel appeared in 1895.

He married an Englishwoman, and in 1898, with his young family, settled in Kent at Pent Farm in Postling, a hamlet near Hythe. Ford Madox Ford, author of *The Good Soldier* and *Parade's End*, had been the previous tenant. Conrad said, looking out from his home over the Romney Marsh towards the sea, 'this is the view I love best in the world'. During his time there, he regularly exchanged visits with H.G. Wells, then living at nearby Sandgate. In 1907, the lease on Pent Farm expired and after a few nomadic years, Conrad finally moved to his last home, Oswalds in Bishopsbourne.

He spent the last five years of his life in the village, dying there on 3 August 1924, and was buried in Canterbury Cemetery, under a misspelled version of his original Polish name, as 'Joseph Teador Conrad

The village hall in Bishopsbourne was renamed after Conrad's death and the commemorative porch added, paid for 'by numerous friends and admirers throughout the world', according to an inscription above the door. (Anne Thompson)

Korzeniowski'. Inscribed on his gravestone are the lines from Spenser's *The Faerie Queen* which he had chosen as the epigraph to his last complete novel, *The Rover*:

Sleep after toyle, port after stormie seas,
Ease after warre, death after life, doth greatly please.

Oswalds still stands and Bishopsbourne village hall is called Conrad Hall in his honour. His family donated to Canterbury Museum some of his furniture and personal items. A re-creation there of his study includes his writing table, typewriter, favourite pen, chess set and hatbox. Also on display is a bronze bust of Conrad made by Sir Jacob Epstein in 1924, a few months before the writer died.

Charles Darwin, naturalist and geologist

Charles Darwin moved his young wife and two small children out of London, which he loathed, and into the clean air and peace of Kent in 1842. They had bought Down House in the village of Downe, near Farnborough. The quiet village was away from main roads, the local scenery beautiful and there were plenty of footpaths on which the energetic Darwin could ramble.

Here he wrote *On the Origin of Species* and *The Descent of Man* as well as works on the huge range of subjects which he studied: insectivorous plants, vegetable mould, different types of fertilisation in plants, earthworms, movement in plants, orchids and the expression of emotions in man and animals. The house became a giant laboratory for researching his theories.

He paid local children to collect seeds and snake and lizard eggs, and neighbouring farmers delivered various dead animals to him. He boiled up wild and domestic ducks to compare their skeletons and then conducted the same experiments on pigeons which he kept in a specially built aviary (although he said that he hated to kill them). Instead of boiling their delicate bodies he dissolved their flesh in a mixture of potash and silver oxide. The smell was appalling and their skeletons lay everywhere throughout the house, until even he admitted it was becoming a chamber of horrors and eventually arranged to have the bodies skeletonised professionally. He tested his theories on seaborne dispersal of species by growing seeds in saltwater on the mantelpiece and conducted experiments on purple loosestrife in the greenhouse and on orchids in the hothouse.

Eight more children were born to Darwin and his wife Emma at Down House. Next to the house he created a wood with a gravel path around the perimeter, the sandwalk path. Here he encouraged his children to observe nature, particularly the habits of bumble bees. Darwin's daily walk of several circuits of this path served both for exercise and for uninterrupted thinking. He set up a number of small stones at one point on the walk so that he could kick a stone to the side each time he passed and not have to interrupt his thoughts by consciously counting the number of circuits he had made that day.

Charles Darwin died at the house on 19 April 1882, aged 73, in his wife's arms. His own wish had been to be buried beneath the great yew tree near the lychgate at Downe church, but the Royal Society and public opinion insisted that he should lie in Westminster Abbey, quite an achievement for a man who was openly agnostic. Emma, however, lies there, together with her infant children.

Charles Dickens, author

Dickens first came to Kent when he was 4 years old, to Chatham, where he lived for the next seven years. Here he was taken to the nearby Theatre Royal in Rochester and was transfixed. He loved it all: the smell of sawdust, lamp-oil and orange peel; the bad, and occasionally good, acting; the costumes; the rickety scenery; even the 'flea-haunted single tier of boxes'. His love of the stage never left him.

Later in life he returned to the county. In his mid-twenties, *The Pickwick Papers* just published, Dickens visited Broadstairs, a seaside resort between Ramsgate and Margate and took lodgings in the High Street. He was to return to the town again and again, and it was in Broadstairs that he found much of the inspiration for one of his most famous characters – Miss Betsey Trotwood, David Copperfield's aunt. In what is now the Dickens House Museum in the town lived Miss Mary Pearson, who according to the reminiscences of Dickens's son Charlie, was a kindly and charming old lady who fed him tea and cakes. He also remembered that she was firmly convinced of her right to stop the passage of donkeys along the cliff top in front of her cottage.

Dickens used the donkey incident for the character of Betsey Trotwood, and described her cottage, with its square gravelled garden full of flowers, and parlour with its old-fashioned furniture, through the eyes of young David Copperfield, although in the novel its location was moved to Dover.

Later, as an established author, Dickens was delighted during one of his strolls to see a 'For Sale' board on a house in Higham, between Gravesend and Rochester. It was not the first time he had seen the place. As a child of 9, he had admired the handsome building and his father had told him that if he worked hard enough, one day he could own it.

He had worked hard and now he bought the house, Gadshill Place, for £1,700. He moved his family in to their new summer residence in 1857.

The family consisted of his wife, his sister-in-law, two daughters and seven sons, but was about to be torn apart. One son embarked almost immediately for India where he died without seeing his father again. The following year, Dickens separated from his wife of over twenty years, Catherine. He was by then conducting an affair with Ellen Tiernan, an actress. They often, through necessity – Dickens's reputation as a family man could not be tarnished – met in France, and on one of these occasions, when travelling back from Dover by train to London, their train was derailed near Staplehurst. Ten passengers were killed, and Dickens subsequently developed a fear of train journeys and indeed any travel, which stayed with him until his death.

Dickens loved to entertain at Gadshill Place, and guests were taken out on walks and excursions in the neighborhood, to Rochester Castle, to Maidstone, to Canterbury Cathedral and to Cooling churchyard. Here, the dozen lozenge-shaped graves inspired the monuments to Pip's five dead

Dickens often took his visitors for picnics in the churchyard of St James's church in Cooling. The little graves belong to the children of two families, aged between 1 month and 2 years who died in the late eighteenth and nineteenth centuries. (Anne Thompson)

little brothers in the opening scene of *Great Expectations*. With a ruined castle opposite and the bleak flat marsh leading towards the sea, it is easy to imagine Magwich lurking behind a gravestone.

In June 1870, after a particularly arduous round of public reading engagements, he returned to Gadshill Place where he was trying to finish *The Mystery of Edwin Drood*. On 8 June, at dinner, he complained of feeling unwell. Doctors attended, but Dickens lay unconscious until the evening of the next day, when he breathed his last.

Not long before his death he had spoken of Gadshill Place to an acquaintance: 'I love the dear old place; and I hope – when I come to die – it may be there.' In this he got his wish, but his instructions for his funeral were ignored. He wanted no 'monument, memorial or testimonial', but instead an unseemly tussle developed between Rochester Cathedral and Westminster Abbey as to who would receive his body. Celebrity tombs, then as now, meant visitors, which meant additional income. Westminster Abbey won.

William Harvey, physician

William Harvey was born to a prosperous, land-owning yeoman family in 'a fair stone house' in Folkestone on 1 April 1578. He was the first son of Thomas Harvey, a jurat (town councillor) and later mayor of the town, and his second wife Joan, described on her memorial plaque in the church of St Mary and St Eanswythe in the town as 'a godly harmless woman'. William was followed by six brothers and two sisters, all of whom, remarkably for the time, survived childhood. The sisters married well and the brothers were all successful, either at Court or in business.

William's elementary education was probably at a church school, but at the age of 10 he was admitted to the King's School, Canterbury, one of the oldest schools in England. The education provided was predominantly religious and classical, with a focus on Latin and a little Greek. After school, he attended Caius College, Cambridge. He then studied medicine at the University of Padua, where he was taught by the physician Hieronymus Fabricius.

Fabricius, who was fascinated by anatomy, recognised that the veins in the human body had one-way valves, but was puzzled as to their function. It was Harvey who took the foundation of Fabricius's teaching, and went on to solve the riddle of what part the valves played in the circulation of blood through the body.

On his return from Italy in 1602, Harvey established himself in medical practice. In 1607, he became a fellow of the Royal College of Physicians and, in 1609, was appointed physician to St Bartholomew's Hospital. In 1618, he became physician to Elizabeth's successor James I and to James's son Charles when he became king. Both James and Charles took a close interest in and encouraged Harvey's research.

He first revealed his findings to the College of Physicians in 1616, and in 1628 he published his theories in a book, *Exercitatio Anatomica de Motu Cordis et Sanguinis in Animalibus* (An Anatomical Study of the Motion of the Heart and of the Blood in Animals), explaining for the first time how the heart propelled the blood in a circular course through the body. His discovery was received with great interest in England, although there were those who thought he was mad.

Harvey was also the first to suggest that humans and other mammals reproduced via the fertilisation of an egg by sperm. It took a further two centuries before a mammalian egg was finally observed, but nonetheless Harvey's theory won credibility during his lifetime.

A statue of William Harvey in Folkestone, the town of his birth. He holds a heart in his left hand, and his right hand is placed over his own heart. (Anne Thompson)

William Harvey inherited the family home in Folkestone when his father died and bequeathed it to Caius College, his alma mater. He himself died childless in 1657, at the home of his brother Eliab in Roehampton. The NHS hospital in Ashford is named for him, as is the grammar school in Folkestone, founded by his nephew and executor, Eliab.

Derek Jarman, artist, designer and film-maker

In 1986, Derek Jarman was lunching in Dungeness with friends and decided to visit the old lighthouse. Admiring a nearby fisherman's cottage, he told his companions that were it ever for sale, he would buy it. As they drew nearer, they saw the 'For Sale' sign, and so, with money left to him by his father, Jarman bought Prospect Cottage. It was to be his home until his death, and the site of a garden that was as innovative as the rest of his art.

Dungeness is the only area of the United Kingdom designated as a desert because of its aridity and lack of surface vegetation and it is blasted by gales in winter. Prospect Cottage, a simple wooden dwelling, lies almost in the middle, overlooked by the nuclear power station. It was not, on the face of it, the ideal place to make a garden.

Using only what will tolerate the hostile conditions, Jarman used sea kale, gorse, broom, herbs, valerian and sea thrift, excavating huge quantities of sea shingle to make planting possible. Plants were surrounded by ad hoc sculptures, some found objects, some assembled, made of anything the area could produce, including the heads of old garden tools, the balls of metal floats, chains, anchors, hooks and wartime fence posts with spiral ends for threading barbed wire. He collected stones with holes in them and strung them together like necklaces which were draped and hung around the site.

Jarman was already ill when he bought Prospect Cottage, and the garden came to have a new meaning for him – the plants battling against the devastating winds seemed to represent his own struggle with ill-health. The garden, however, blossomed, while Jarman faded.

Jarman's work in other media was transformed by his Dungeness experience. His canvases were coated in tar or pitch into which glass or mirrors

Admirers of Derek Jarman place stones on his gravestone at St Clement's church in Old Romney, perhaps as reminders of his celebrated garden on Dungeness. (Anne Thompson)

were placed and then smashed, and he also painted views of Dungeness or the marshland surrounding the area. In 1990, he made one of his last films, *The Garden*, which was based on his own home movies of his Dungeness home interspersed with improvised sequences on the theme of the Gospels.

Jarman died in 1994 of complications arising from AIDS.

Augustus Pugin, architect

When Augustus Welby Northmore Pugin moved to Ramsgate in 1844 at the age of 32, he was already a national figure. As an architect, designer and author, he had changed the course of the Gothic revival movement in

England and had designed the interior of the new Houses of Parliament, the stained glass, metalwork, wood carving, upholstery, furniture and a royal throne. The speed at which he worked was legendary: in one month in 1843, two churches and a cathedral had been completed and he was well known enough to be satirised in *Punch*.

The Grange, the house he built for himself and his children in Ramsgate, was less whimsical than some of his earlier designs, and comprised a family home within an inner courtyard, although it was thought a controversial design at the time. There was a little chapel projecting to the east, and a tower with battlements, which housed water tanks, and gave wonderful views of the sea Pugin loved. In the magnificent library he had his drawing board by the bay window and here he worked, interrupted only by daily mass in the chapel (he was a Catholic convert), food and a daily walk.

Here he designed the medieval court for the Great Exhibition of 1851, and the Catholic Southwark Cathedral, in which he was the first person to be married, to his third wife, in 1848. More controversially, he built a Catholic church next to The Grange, a move which agitated the moderate Anglicans of Ramsgate so much that they employed the other great Gothic revival architect of the day, George Gilbert Scott, to build them a new church, too.

At the end of Pugin's life, in February 1852, he supplied a detailed design for the iconic Westminster Palace clock tower, officially dubbed the Elizabeth Tower, but known throughout the world as Big Ben. Later that same month he was taken ill while travelling to London by train. After a period in various asylums, his wife brought him home to Ramsgate, where he died aged only 40, on 14 September 1852. He is buried in his church, St Augustine's, next to his house.

Vita Sackville-West, writer and gardener

Vita Sackville-West first saw Sissinghurst Castle, near Cranbrook, in 1930. She said later it was 'the Sleeping Beauty's castle with a vengeance', and she fell in love with it, despite its almost complete dilapidation. Her husband, Harold Nicholson, former diplomat and now a journalist, also saw its potential and despite warnings from family and friends, they bought it. Their marriage was an unconventional arrangement in which both Vita and Harold took lovers, but Sissinghurst was to become the joint venture of their lives.

They spent a small fortune restoring the place. In the entrance range, a library was created, and the tower became Vita's private sanctuary where she wrote. She stripped the Victorian wallpaper, had electricity connected, and in its octagonal turret she had a small personal library.

Vita and Harold started laying out the garden in 1932, after two years of planning and clearance work. They planted lime trees, yews salvaged from Penshurst churchyard, a hornbeam hedge; they made a lake, created a nuttery and planted wisteria and delphiniums and polyanthus, working side-by-side in the muddy beds. Three gardeners were employed and by the late 1930s Vita's and Harold's complementary outlooks – his classical, hers romantic – had transformed Sissinghurst's 2.5 hectares into the now famous garden.

It is designed as a series of 'rooms', each with a different character of colour or theme. Harold was largely responsible for making interconnections between the 'rooms', while Vita worked on the planting schemes. It was opened for the first time, under the National Garden Scheme, in 1938. The admission fee was a shilling, and visitors left their coins in an old tobacco tin on a table by the entrance archway. Vita called the paying guests 'shillingses'.

Vita enjoyed considerable commercial success during her early years at Sissinghurst, writing *The Edwardians* and *All Passion Spent*, and became something of a local celebrity. Her appearance as guest of honour at speech day at Tonbridge County School for Girls inspired cheering and autograph hunting. The horrified headmistress deplored such 'unwarranted and vulgar scenes'.

In 1946, Vita started writing a regular garden column for *The Observer*. It won her renewed popularity and her weekly mailbag sometimes contained 2,000 letters from readers. Her contribution to gardening was recognised and honoured by the Royal Horticultural Society and Sissinghurst was visited by royalty.

Vita died at her Kent home in 1962. Five years later Sissinghurst was given by the Nicholson family into the care of the National Trust.

John Tradescant senior and junior, gardeners and botanists

John Tradescant the elder, a Suffolk man by birth, had by his middle years become a fashionable gardener, and in 1615 was taken on by Edward, Lord Wotton, to work at St Augustine's Abbey in Canterbury. A small royal palace had been built on the ruins of the abbey and Wotton rented it as a second home. There Tradescant created for him a garden of 8 to 12 hectares filled with 'orchards, sweet walks, labyrinth-like wildernesses and groves, rare mounts and fountains', and kept a kitchen garden which supplied the lord's table with delicacies such as melons. This new post was a step down from Tradescant's previous position at Hatfield House, but Wotton allowed him complete artistic freedom and Tradescant filled the garden with the rare plants he had collected from the Alps, Sardinia, Morocco, Persia, Russia and Corsica, including anemones, pinks and roses. After Canterbury, he went on to work for George Villiers, first Duke of Buckingham and favourite of James I, and later for Charles I.

He gave his son, also John, the classical education he lacked, and sent him to the King's School in Canterbury. There the boy learnt the Latin which would enable him to construct names for the strange new plants he would discover.

His father had travelled in Europe, but John junior went further afield, to Virginia, to collect plants. Among the seeds he brought back were those of trees and plants which are now staples of the English garden: magnolias, cypress, the tulip tree, phlox and asters.

When his father died he succeeded as head gardener to Charles I and Henrietta Maria, designing and planting the gardens at Inigo Jones's Queen's House in Greenwich. He was left unemployed when the queen fled to France during the Civil War, but instead compiled and published the contents of his father's collection of curiosities: books, exotic plants, mineral specimens, coins, weapons, costumes, taxidermy, and other ephemera. The collection was priceless, and on Tradescant's death it passed to Elias Ashmole, another collector, under circumstances which did not leave the latter smelling of roses. However, it formed the core of the Ashmolean Museum in Oxford where it remains largely intact.

John Tradescant junior was buried beside his father in the churchyard of St-Mary-at-Lambeth, which is now established as the Museum of Garden History.

H.G. Wells, author

Herbert George Wells was born in Bromley, Kent, in 1866 in humble surroundings over a shop in the High Street. His father sold crockery and cricketing paraphernalia to supplement an erratic income earned as a professional cricketer and coach. After school, Wells had several false career starts before becoming a teacher. Married young to a first cousin, he left his wife to live with one of his students in Sevenoaks, causing a local scandal. During this period he wrote his first novel, *The Time Machine*, published in 1895.

Four years later, now respectably married to his former mistress, he set out on a tandem ride with her through Kent and Sussex. Arriving in Sandgate, he was taken ill, and was obliged to stay there. During his prolonged convalescence at 'Beach Cottage' on the sea front, he decided that it was the perfect place to settle down, but failing to find a suitable house, he built one, Spade House, a little further along the coast. He

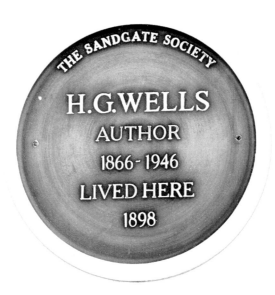

A plaque on Beach Cottage on the seafront at Sandgate commemorates the tenancy of H.G. Wells. He said that in rough weather, the waves broke over the roof of the house. (Anne Thompson)

employed the architect C.F.A. Voysey, but the building work was interrupted repeatedly by their running arguments. The architect usually left a signature heart shape on the front door of every home he designed, but Wells, never a conformist, insisted that the heart be replaced by the ace of spades. Furthermore, he wanted every door in the house to have the same motif. Voysey thought this was expensive, time-consuming and vulgar. Wells sacked him and brought in another builder who did what he wanted. The house cost close to £3,000, a small fortune. Wells needed to earn money, and *The First Men on the Moon* and *Love and Mr Lewisham* were the results.

Wells and his wife lived at Spade House for the next ten years, and their two sons were born there. Wells, however, never much of a family man, also rented a small flat in London from 1902, where he met his left-wing friends and started an affair with Amber Reeves. He told friends he was going to sell Spade House and get a divorce, but his accommodating wife tolerated his extra-marital relationships and even allowed Wells to move her out of Spade House and up to Hampstead to leave Spade House available for him and his mistress. Wells finally lost interest in Amber, and the house was sold. There were other books and other mistresses, but Wells did not return to Kent.

James Wolfe, soldier

James Wolfe was born in 1727 at the vicarage in Westerham. Around 1738, the Wolfe family moved to Greenwich. From his earliest years, Wolfe was destined for a military career, entering his father's 1st Marine Regiment as a volunteer at the age of 13. Although of relatively humble birth, unlike many of his colleagues, once commissioned, his rise was rapid. He saw service in the War of the Austrian Succession, and the Jacobite rebellion and during the Seven Years War he was sent to Canada. William Pitt, the prime minister, had chosen to strike at the enemy, France, through her Canadian possessions and the key to these was Quebec. He chose James Wolfe to lead the attack on the city, promoting him to the rank of major-general. He was only 32 years old.

After a three-month siege, Wolfe led a bold but risky amphibious landing at the base of the cliffs west of Quebec along the St Lawrence river. His army, with two small cannon, scaled the cliffs from the river below early in the morning of 13 September 1759, surprising the French, who thought the feat impossible. In the ensuing battle, the French were soon defeated, but when Wolfe began to move forward, he was shot three times, in the arm, the shoulder and the chest. As he lay dying, he was told that the French were on the run, and spoke his final words: 'God be praised, I die contented.'

Death transformed Wolfe into a national hero, an image encouraged by Benjamin West's iconic portrayal of his death as modern-day martyrdom. The painting was, rather oddly, presented by the British Government to Canada in 1921 in recognition of their assistance during the First World War. His childhood home has been preserved in his memory by the National Trust under the name 'Quebec House'.

A statue of Wolfe on the green at Westerham, alongside that of one of the village's other famous resident, Sir Winston Churchill. Another overlooks the Royal Naval College in Greenwich. (Anne Thompson)

FURTHER READING

Berg, Mary and Howard Jones, *Norman Churches in the Canterbury Diocese*, Stroud: The History Press, 2009

Boyle, John, *Portrait of Canterbury*, London: Phillimore, 1980

Brookes, Stuart and Sue Harrington, *The Kingdom and People of Kent AD 400–1066*, Stroud: The History Press, 2010

Chalkin, C.W., *Seventeenth Century Kent*, London: John Hallewell, 1965

Coren, Michael, *The Invisible Man: The Life and Liberties of H.G. Wells*, London: Bloomsbury, 1993

Dennison, Matthew, *Behind the Mask: The Life of Vita Sackville-West*, London: Collins, 2014

Detsicas, Alex, *The Cantiaci*, Kent: Sutton, 1983

Filmer, Richard, *Hops and Hop Picking*, Risborough: Shire Publications, 1998

George, Michael and Martin, *Coast of Conflict: The Story of the South Kent Coast*, Sussex: SB Publications, 2004

Hagger, Mark, *William, Conqueror and King*, London: IB Taurus, 2012

Higginbotham, Peter, *A Grim Almanac of the Workhouse*, Stroud: The History Press, 2013

Hill, Derek Ingram, *The Ancient Hospitals and Almshouses of Canterbury*, Canterbury: Canterbury Archaeological Society, 1969

Hill, Rosemary, *God's Architect: Pugin and the Building of Romantic Britain*, London: Penguin, 2007

Ingleton, Roy, *Fortress Kent*, Yorkshire: Pen and Sword, 2012

Ingleton, Roy, *Policing Kent 1800–2000: Guarding the Garden of England*, Trowbridge: Phillimore, 2002

Jarman, Derek, *Derek Jarman's Garden*, London: Thames and Hudson, 1995

Jarvis, Margaret A., *Captain Webb and 100 Years of Channel Swimming*, London: David and Charles, 1975

Johnson, Stephen, *The Roman Forts of the Saxon Shore*, London: HarperCollins, 1976

Keith-Lucas, Bryan, *Parish Affairs: The Government of Kent Under George III*, Kent: Kent County Council, 1986

Klopper, Harry, *To Fire Committed: The History of Fire-Fighting in Kent*, Tonbridge: Kent Council of the FSNBF,1984

Lansberry, Frederick ed., *Government and Politics in Kent, 1640–1914*, Kent: Boydell, 2001

Lawson, Terence and David Killingray eds, *An Historical Atlas of Kent*, Andover: Phillimore, 2010

Leach, Derek, *Dover Harbour: Royal Gateway*, Dover: Riverdale Publications, 2005

Major, Alan, *The Kentish Lights*, Sussex: SB Publications, 2000

McDine, David, *Unconquered: The Story of Kent and its Lieutenancy*, Kent: Allan Willett Foundation, 2014

Melling, Elizabeth, ed., *Kentish Sources VI: Crime and Punishment*, Maidstone: Kent County Council, 1969

Neame, Alan, *The Holy Maid of Kent: The Life of Elizabeth Barton, 1506–1534*, London: Hodder and Stoughton, 1971

Ogley, Bob, *Kent at War*, Kent: Froglets Publications, 1994

Oliver, Neil, *The Vikings*, London: Weidenfeld and Nicholson, 2012

O'Neill, Gilda, *Pull No More Bines*, London: The Women's Press, 1990

Potter, Jennifer, *Strange Blooms: The Curious Lives and Adventures of the John Tradescants*, London: Atlantic Books, 2006

Prestwich, Michael, *Plantagenet England, 1225–1360*, Oxford: Oxford University Press, 2005

Roake, Margaret and John Whyman, eds, *Essays in Kentish History*, London: Frank Cass, 1976

Ruderman, Arthur, *A Short History of Ashford*, Chichester: Phillimore, 1994

Scurrell, David, *The Book of Margate*, Buckingham: Barracuda Books, 1984

Sweetinburgh, Sheila, ed., *Later Medieval Kent*, Suffolk: Boydell and Brewer, 2010

Ungerson, Clare, *Four Thousand Lives: The Rescue of German Jewish Men to Britain, 1939*, Stroud: The History Press, 2014

Venning, Timothy, *The Kings and Queens of Anglo-Saxon England*, Stroud: Amberley, 2013

Waugh, Mary, *Smuggling in Kent and Sussex, 1700–1740*, Newbury: Countryside Books, 1965

Whyman, John, *The Early Kentish Seaside*, Gloucester: The History Press, 1985

Yates, Nigel, Robert Hume and Paul Hastings, *Religion and Society in Kent, 1640–1914*, Kent: Boydell and Brewer, 1994

Zell, Michael, ed., *Early Modern Kent 1540–1640*, Suffolk: Boydell Press, 2000

Ziegler, Philip, *The Black Death*, London: HarperCollins, 1969

ABOUT THE AUTHOR

ANNE PETRIE lives in Hythe, Kent, and has an MA in History. A retired civil servant, she is passionate about local history and chairs the Hythe Local History Group and regularly contributes articles to magazines and parish reviews in Kent.

INDEX